MIX
Papier aus verantwortungsvollen Quellen
Paper from responsible sources
FSC® C105338

Hedwig Heerdt

Green Banks

The fairy tale of sustainability

Anchor Academic
Publishing

Heerdt, Hedwig: Green Banks – The fairy tale of sustainability. Hamburg, Anchor Academic Publishing 2013

Buch-ISBN: 978-3-95489-144-3
PDF-eBook-ISBN: 978-3-95489-644-8
Druck/Herstellung: Anchor Academic Publishing, Hamburg, 2013

Bibliografische Information der Deutschen Nationalbibliothek:
Die Deutsche Nationalbibliothek verzeichnet diese Publikation in der Deutschen Nationalbibliografie; detaillierte bibliografische Daten sind im Internet über http://dnb.d-nb.de abrufbar.

Bibliographical Information of the German National Library:
The German National Library lists this publication in the German National Bibliography. Detailed bibliographic data can be found at: http://dnb.d-nb.de

Hermannstal 119k, 22119 Hamburg
http://www.diplomica-verlag.de, Hamburg 2013
Printed in Germany

I Abstract

Because Ethical Banks have developed from niche players to serious competition for traditional banks, supposedly Ethical Banks and even traditional banks use the term Ethical Bank in order to sell bank services under the cloak of sustainable and ethically correct business conduct.

Therefore, the focus of this research is to make truly Ethical Banks distinguishable from traditional banks by investigating, analysing and determining principles, Ethical Banks have to fulfil or refrain from in order to call themselves truly ethical. Based on academic research results, a web-based survey identifies bank customer's attitude towards sustainability, ethics, their banking and ethical attitude towards nine areas of business, banks may be confronted with. The survey result build the basis for a list of positive and negative Ethical Guiding Principles, which should serve as a general standard for Ethical Banks.

But because of the ever-changing environmental, social and legal environment, EGPs need to be continuously reviewed and validated. If directly implemented, a control mechanism within or outside the bank must monitor and ensure compliance with these principles.

II Table of contents

III Table of figures

IV List of tables

V List of abbreviations

EEA

(= European Economic Area) The EEA compromises all EU member states, as well as Iceland, Liechtenstein and Norway, since they entered into the EEA Agreement in January 1994. Even though Switzerland was one of the founding member of EFTA, later, they did not join the EEA Agreement, but established bilateral agreements with the EU. However, for reasons of simplifications, in the course of this dissertation the term EEA shall refer to Switzerland, as well. (EFTA, 2012a)

EFTA

(= European Free Trade Association) EFTA was founded in 1960 in order to encourage free trade between the Western European countries. Today, EFTA allows Iceland, Liechtenstein and Norway in accordance with the EEA Agreement to take an active part in the European Internal Market. (EFTA, 2012b)

EIRIS

(= Ethical Investment Research Service) “EIRIS is a leading global provider of research into corporate environmental, social and governance performance” (EIRIS, 2012). Their mission “is to empower responsible investors” (EIRIS, 2012) with their knowledge. For ethically aware consumers they have established investment funds and an advisory website for green and ethical finance (YourEthicalMoney.org, 2012).

FEBEA

(= European Federation of Ethical and Alternative Banks) FEBEA is a non-profit organisation under Belgium law since 2001, compromising 25 member banks. All of their members “share the same concern for transparency and social and environmental utility” (FEBEA, 2012b). Furthermore, “FEBEA aims to create financial tools [..] to help existing European initiatives and encourage the growth of new initiatives in the field of alternative finance“ (FEBEA, 2012b).

Millennium Development Goal

The United Nations Development Programme "partners with people at all levels of society to help build nations that can withstand crisis, and drive and sustain the kind of growth that improves the quality of life for everyone. On the ground in 177 countries and territories, [..] [they] offer global perspective and local insight to help empower lives and build resilient nations" (UNEP, 2012a). Until 2015, the Millennium Development Goals aim to eradicate poverty and hunger, achieve universal education, promote gender equality, improve child and maternal health, combat HIV/AIDS, malaria and other diseases, ensure environmental sustainability and develop a global partnership for development (United Nations, 2012).

UNEP

(= United Nations Environment Programme) "The United Nations Environment Programme (UNEP) is an international organization established in 1972 to catalyse and coordinate activities to increase scientific understanding of environmental change and develop environmental management tools" (OECD, 2012). UNEP's areas of interest are: Climate change, disasters and conflicts, ecosystem management, environmental governance, harmful substances and resource efficiency (UNEP, 2012c).

1 Introduction

1.1 Background

"A business that makes nothing but money is a poor business."

Henry Ford (1903)

Histories of companies show that Ford (1903) was right - solely profit-oriented considerations do not suffice to make a company successful. Ever since, companies were "increasingly expected [...] to improve their competitive advantage by demonstrating economic progress while maintaining environmental care and social responsibility" (Arsov, 2008).

Although Jeucken (2002b, p. 1) stated that "humankind's awareness of its dependence of the environment goes back to the very beginning of human history", it was not before the 1980s that Western societies realised that the environment has become an issue of increasing concern (Gerrans & Hutchinson, 2000, p. 75; Robbins, 2001, p. 3).

Besides, because of the subprime crisis, bank customer's confidence levels worldwide have changed severely. According to Ernst & Young (2011, pp. 2-7), banks experience challenges in maintaining customer relationships due to crisis impacts on trust levels. Especially European banks are affected by decreasing trust and confidence levels, as bank customers look for alternatives to traditional banks.

Considering the lack of consumer trust, in conjunction with changing social demand towards social and environmental responsibility and increasing awareness of customers about ethical and community-oriented banking, traditional banks generally cannot satisfy these demands (Kleanthous & Peck, 2006, p. 31; Goyal & Joshi, 2011, p. 53).

In fact, according to experts like Burrett (UNEP), traditional banks are "very much on the back foot" (Bloomberg, 2011) with green projects and regard ethical behaviour as "little more than a bolt-on to normal operations" (Street & Monaghan, 2011, p. 72). Hence, customers turned to Ethical Banks, which as a result "transformed [...] from niche institutions to large, publicly visible players" (Goyal & Joshi, 2011, p. 53).

1.2 Research focus

Although the financial crisis may have strengthened the demand for Ethical Banks, little consideration is given so far to ethics in finance and particularly to ethics in banks, so that it is a research subject to develop nowadays (Boatright, 2008, p. 7).

Additionally, customers struggle to identify truly Ethical Banks because there is no such certificate, quality seal or standardised rating that helps customers assess the ethical quality of a bank. Considering other fields of business, quality seals (432 eco-labels in 246 countries) like the 'CSR-Tourism-certified' seal in the travel industry, are globally accepted and make the identification of ethical services, respectively products customer-friendly and easy (Global Sustainable Tourism Council, 2012; Ecolabel Index, 2012).

National eco-labels like the German 'Blue Angel' or Europe-wide 'EU Ecolabel', set standards for eco-friendly products and services, but fail to include financial services (The Blue Angel, 2012; European Commission, 2012a).

Furthermore, marketing slogans suggesting ethical behaviour like Deutsche Bank's (2012) "Banking on Green" or Lloyds (2012) "Doing more to help Britain prosper" (Lloyds, 2012) may confuse customers in their quest for a truly ethical partner because these banks may not be as ethical after all. UBS serves as an excellent example: While advertising "high ethical standards to all [..] activities and decisions" (UBS, 2011, p. 6) in their 'Code of Business Conduct and Ethics' and being one of the first banks to sign the UNEP Statement, UBS was vigorously criticised for violating social and environmental policies by funding the Turkish Ilisu Dam project (Giuseppi, 2001, p. 102). Ultimately, UBS backed out of the project because of rising stakeholder pressure.

To conclude, advertisements, company policies like Corporate Social Responsibility (CSR), regular environmental reports or banking rules that prohibit certain products or behaviour, do not suffice to make a bank truly ethical (Al-Ajmi, Al-Saleh & Abo Hussain, 2011).

1.3 Research aim and objectives

Because of the high amount of uncertainty surrounding banks' ethical performance, this paper aims to investigate, analyse and determine principles

Ethical Banks have to fulfil or refrain from in order to call themselves truly ethical. These guiding principles should serve as a general standard for Ethical Banks that want to settle down within the European Economic Area (EEA).

Therefore, a web-based survey will identify bank customer's attitude towards sustainability and ethics in general, their banking habits, as well as their ethical attitude towards nine areas of business that banks may be confronted with.

Based on the academic research and survey results, a set of Ethical Guiding Principles will be established to limit banking activities to a predetermined social and environmental framework.

The following analysis focuses on banks in the EEA, as these countries share similar features such as employment and social rights or environmental policies (European Commission, 2012c). Hence, survey results can be applied to banks of the EEA only.

The objectives of this research specifically are:

1. Investigate Ethical Bank's definition and significance;
2. Evaluate critically ethical behaviour as disclosed in environmental reports, Ethical Performance Indicators and Principles;
3. Investigate theories explaining ethical behaviour and decision making;
4. Examine critically bank customer's opinion towards Ethical Banks in general and determine Ethical Guiding Principles that are most relevant to them;
5. Formulate negative and positive criteria so that Ethical Banks can conduct their business accordingly, to be ultimately rewarded with the title 'Ethical Bank'.

This research will contribute to Ethical Bank's development in a number of ways: first by providing a critical review of issues pertinent to Ethical Banks; second by critically examining Environmental Reporting standards to identify potential problems when comparing reports; third by introducing ethical metrics to raise awareness of the great potential hidden in this tool; fourth by reviewing existing theories of ethical decision making, allowing a meaningful study result interpretation from which behavioural standards for Ethical Banks can be derived.

But not only is this research relevant for banks, it is useful for retail bank customers searching for a bank that makes the triple-bottom-line a reality, but without requiring them to actively evaluate a bank's ethical standards.

1.4 Outline structure

The research is structured as follows:

Chapter 1: Introduction

This first chapter provides the reader with background information on Ethical Banks and highlights their development. After that, the focus of this research is discussed and justified; and the overall research aim and individual research objectives are identified.

Chapter 2: Literature Review

The Literature Review defines the term Ethical Bank, discusses the role of banks in the economy and identifies stages of sustainability. Furthermore, issues surrounding Environmental Reporting, Ethical Performance Measurement and Ethical Guiding Principles undertaken by EEA banks with ethical business expertise, will be contrasted with existing literature. To conclude, the ethical decision-making will be discussed in the context of individuals and businesses.

Chapter 3: Theoretical framework

The third chapter explains the basis of the research problems and explains the theoretical phenomena upon which the study tries to fill gaps in the existing literature and banking practice.

Chapter 4: Data and methodology

Taking a post-positivist stance, this chapter draws up the quantitative research conducted in the course of this study. Therefore the planning, development and execution of the survey will be explained, as well as the analysis of data. Subsequently, research issues will be discussed.

Chapter 5: Findings and analysis of results

This chapter elaborates the survey findings and discusses them critically in the context of the concepts outlined in the Literature Review.

Chapter 6: Conclusion

Chapter 6 summarises the main research findings. It outlines the contributions of the findings and offers suggestions for future research based on the results and limitations of this project.

2 Literature Review

This chapter discusses literature with the aim of investigating Ethical Banks and analysing concepts of disclosing ethical data, performance measurement and guiding principles. Finally, ethical decision-making will be discussed.

2.1 Ethical Banks

According to analysts "the pool of genuinely ethical financial service providers remains small [...] [and] only a handful [...] stick rigidly to a policy of responsible investment" (Goff, 2011).

2.1.1 Definition

Although there is no uniform definition of Ethical Banks, literature refers to them as "sustainable, social, alternative, development or solidarity" (de Clerck, 2009) commercial banks that meet "the needs of the present without compromising the ability of future generations to meet their own needs" (WCED, 1987, p. 41). Bouma, et al. (2001, p. 101) added that it "is a decision by banks to provide products and services [..] to customers who take into consideration the environmental and social impact of their actions". According to Goyal and Joshi (2011, p. 53), it is "the modest way to deal with money than traditional banking".

Summarising those definitions, characteristically are three key factors – social, economic and environmental development. Although, these factors originated in the Treaty of Amsterdam (European Communities, 1997), they describe precisely Ethical Banks as they "not only comprise the natural heritage [..] [they] pass on to the next generation but also the economic achievements and social institutions of [..] society [...]. [Ethical Bank's success] rests on an ecological, an economic and a social pillar. If one of the pillars gives way, the 'sustainability building' will collapse" (Goethe Institut, 2008). However, the extent Ethical Banks have to comply with these pillars remains undefined.

Figure 1: Key factors of Ethical Banking – The triple bottom line

To cope with this problem, FEBEA (2012a) suggests that Ethical Banks "not [only] follow [..] minimum or 'negative' criteria [...] [, but] concrete and positive criteria". However, FEBEA's definition seems very general and focuses mainly on investment policies.

Thus, Barbu and Boitan (2009, p. 470) came up with a list of characteristics for each bank type. According to them, Ethical Banks operate with a clear set of values and know, respect and accept all hierarchical levels. Their goal is to obtain financial and social gains by choosing ethical projects on basis of customer's decision and the degree of positive influence on society and environment. Contrariwise, traditional banks are subordinated to reaching quantitative objectives like profitability. Therefore, they establish investment strategies and risk profiles that lead to the maximisation of financial gains and offer financing without taking into account impacts on the society and the environment.

Stahlmann and Clausen's approach (2000, p. 78) is similar to Barbu and Boitan's, who categorise the customers into two types – homo oeconomicus and homo vitalis. On the one hand, homo oeconomicus is the rational and self-interested investor who aims for maximum profit and capital appropriation. Homo vitalis on the other hand is an investor who aims for closed-loop economies with qualitative growth and supports renewable energies.

According to Cowen, Thompson (1999) and Green (1989) Ethical Banking is based on two characteristics: social and economic profitability. San Jose, et al.

(2011) added a third variable - “the recognition of the institutions as a bank or as a credit institution by national authorities”.

Rodriguez and Cabaleiro (2007, p. 233) criticised Cowen and Thompson because Ethical Banking is seen as a constant variable with a scale from the “philanthropic end based on an exclusive social or ethical approach, to another end based only on financial aspects”. Therefore, they took up Cowen and Thompson’s idea and developed a model with two axes – social and economic covenants – to position banks according to their degree of ethical and economical behaviour.

Bearing these theoretical approaches in mind, one can recognise that these findings are if anything a description, but not a generally accepted definition.

And although there is no standard definition for Ethical Banks, banks not complying with their promulgated ethical policy will be punished by their customers and the media, as seen in the case of Paxbank (Spiegel Online, 2009; Stern, 2009). But, if such information do not surface in public, unethical behaviour from those claiming to be ethical would neither be recognised nor punished.

2.1.2 The role of Ethical Banks

Because of banks’ central role in an economic system, it is crucial to realise their importance in contributing towards sustainable development. Figure 2 shows a simplified macroeconomic cycle in which banks are connected to other market participants by money flows.

Street and Monaghan (2011, p. 73) identified seven partner-groups that are directly involved in the economic cycle of a co-operative bank. Certainly, partner-groups change according to the corporate structure of a bank (Burkhardt, Franzen, & Kumbartzki, 2005), but the high number of partner-groups exemplifies why banks play such an important role in the economy. This is coherent with stakeholder theory that underlines that “paying attention to the needs and rights of all the stakeholders of a business is a useful way of developing ethically responsible behaviour” (Campbell & Kitson, 2008, p. 17).

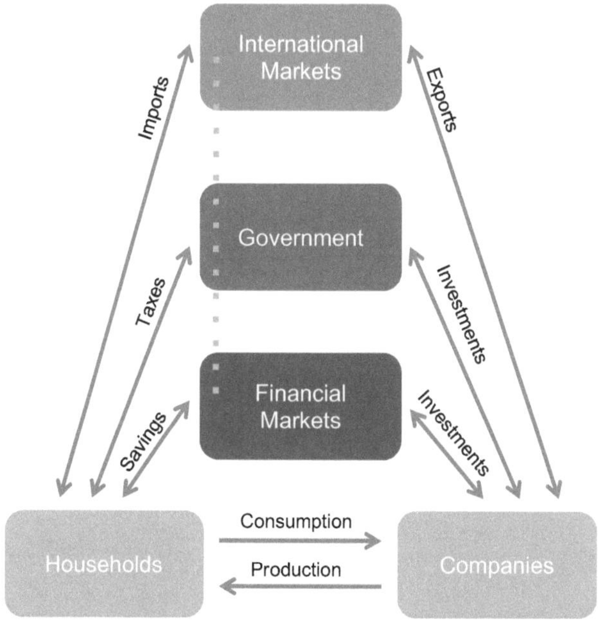

Figure 2: The role of banks in the economy (Jeucken & Bouma, 1999, p.24)

Jeucken and Bouma (1999, pp. 22-24) added that banks have attracted governments and institutions as they can influence the pace and direction of economic growth quantitatively and qualitatively by transforming money by scale, duration, place and assessing, respectively spreading risk in the economy.

According to Bernanke (1983) and New Keynesians, banks can limit asymmetric information because of the ability to assess financial and environmental risk. Banks can ultimately make sure money is lent to 'good' borrowers only (Clary, Dolfsma, & Figart, 2006, p. 43; Thomas, 2006, p. 258).

KPMG (1999, p. 12) stated that the financial sector is generally considered as non-polluting, however their size and position make their impact significant (Jeucken & Bouma, 1999, p. 29; Giuseppi, 2001, p. 103). Indeed, banks are less polluting than manufacturing industries, but indirect effects are substantial (Tarna, 2001, p. 149) since "a bank transforms money into place, term, size and risk in an economy and, as such, it affects [not only] economic development, [but sustainable development]" (Jeucken, 2002b, p. 2).

2.1.3 Stages of sustainability

Despite opportunities ethical behaviour can offer (Sörensen, 2001), banks still find themselves in different stages of sustainability and many have not reached the final level yet, which is required to call oneself Ethical Bank.

According to Bouma, et al. (2001, p. 22) sustainability is a three-stage-process: First, banks are defensive and ignore environmental and social issues. In the next stage banks act more proactively towards sustainability and include ethical issues to a certain degree in their business activities for example by implementing environmental cost savings and eco-efficient procedures. The final stage - sustainability - (where Ethical Banks find themselves in) embraces an ethical corporate philosophy and looks for sustainable rate of returns and long-term profits.

Jeucken (1998, p. 20), Niskala and Mätäsaho (1997) extended Bouma's model (Figure 3) by subdividing the stage of proactivity into preventive (internal integration of ethical procedures) and offensive banking (external measures). This makes a more precise distinction between stages possible. All those models emphasise that with an increase in sustainable awareness, the need for enclosing environmental information rises.

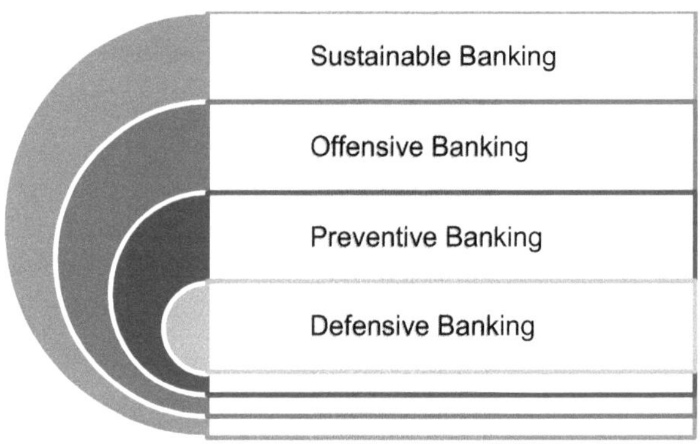

Figure 3: Four stages of sustainable banking (Jeucken, 1998, p. 20)

Figure 4 shows Jeucken's findings by accumulating the results of national banks on country-level. Although, research was carried out nearly 10 years ago, one can see differences in the application of ethical policies and stages of ethical standards banks find themselves in. Hence, issues arise when one tries to distinguish between traditional and Ethical Banks.

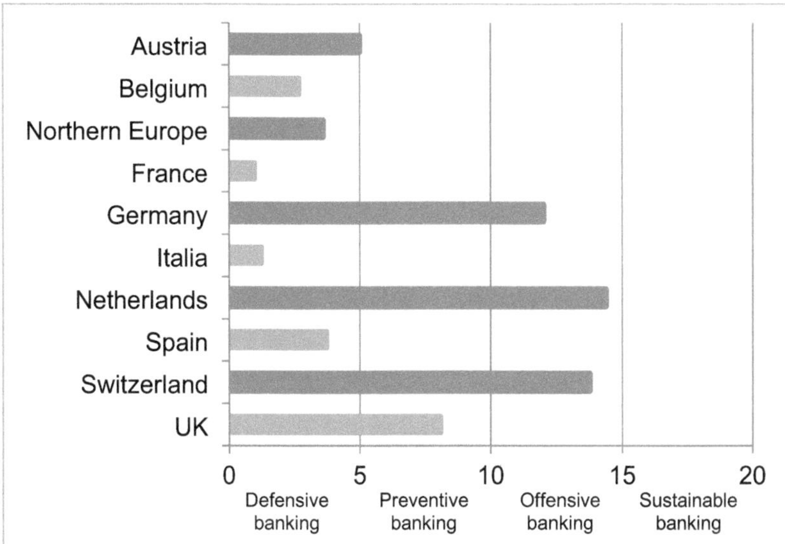

Figure 4: Ethical development of European banks consolidated by country (Jeucken, 2002a, p. 16)

German, Swiss and Dutch banks (Figure 5) make it even harder because they already implemented high degrees of ethical and environmental awareness into their business programs.

Figure 4 also shows that 10 years ago the average of investigated banks had not reached the level of sustainability. Taking the 2012 Environmental Performance Index into consideration (analogue to Millenium Development Goals) where EEA countries rank within the Top 50, corporations have experiences a rapid positive development of sustainability and ethics (Yale Center for Environmental Law & Policy, 2012, p. 10).

Therefore, "in order to investigate the rigour of the approach taken [by EEA's Ethical Banks], we have to get beyond the marketing and into the method by which the investment [and lending] philosophy is applied" (O'Rourke, 2003).

Thus, the next chapter will focus on Environmental Reporting.

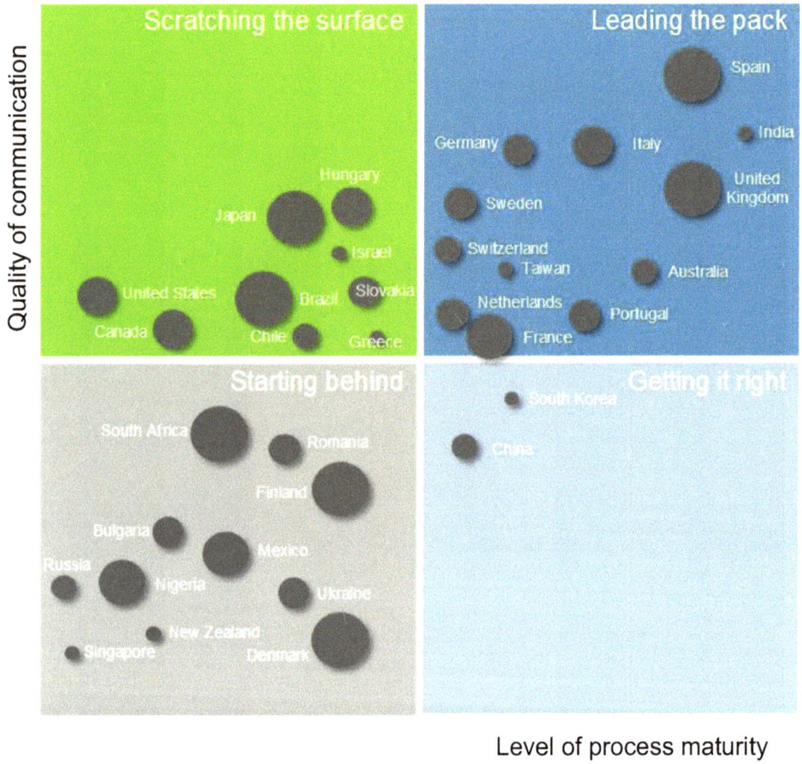

Figure 5: KPMG Corporate Reporting Quadrants 2011 (based on countries) (KPMG, 2011, p. 4)

2.2 Measuring social and environmental development

2.2.1 Environmental Reporting

Unlike financial information, there are neither standard Environmental Reporting guidelines, nor a universally accepted definition of sustainable reporting (KPMG, 2008, p. 8). In comparison to financial reports, environmental reports differ in many ways because there "are no required contents or presentation styles" (Lober, et al., 1997, p. 62). And while researchers criticised a decade ago that banks encourage short-term goals only, today there are several reporting guidelines by different institutions, reflecting the urge for ethical behaviour in the financial service industry. 'Sustainable Reporting Guidelines' being the most common (Schmidheiny & Zorraquin, 1996, p. 4; Tarna, 2001).

In general, each approach has different strengths and weaknesses, and according to Lober, et al. (1997, p. 62) corporate environmental reports differ by the amount of quantitative and qualitative disclosure, the degree of interaction between the reader and the report, and "the reports' ability to convey an evolution in corporate performance over time" (Lober, et al., 1997, p. 62).

Cultural differences seem to be a further differentiating factor. Jeucken (2002a, p. 13) discovered that there is "conformity within a country [...], [but] while the economy is global, [...] peer pressure appears confined within nation borders".

However, certain similarities are striking in all reports (Dias-Sardinha, et al., 2007, p. 16):

- "[The] use of qualitative and/or quantitative indicators [...],
- clustering of indicators into categories [...], and
- [the] use of structural information that may be organized in frameworks."

Against this background, Henriques and Richardson (2004, p. 72f.) outlined that poor standardisation means that stakeholders - including customers – cannot comprehend the extent organisations act environmentally and socially responsible because in many cases these reports just don't make "sense when taken out of the context of capitalism, local laws and culture [...], the state and the functioning of wider environmental systems" (Henriques & Richardson, 2004, p. 72f.).

It seems clear that simply requiring banks to disclose environmental information will not help stakeholders to make informed decisions on ethical bank behaviour.

2.2.2 Ethical Performance Measurement

Because stakeholders have difficulties making decisions on Ethical Banks, Stigson (1999, p. 6) proposed to include metrics to measure ethical behaviour. Since environmental reports suffer from a lack of comparability, ethical metrics set in proportion to economic indicators can help maintaining credibility, prepare qualitative and quantitative ethical data in a comprehensible way and help converting data into conclusive and concise information about ethical performance.

Bartolomeo (1995) defines metrics as "quantitative and qualitative information that allow the evaluation [...] of [a] company['s] effectiveness and efficiency" with respect to social and environmental aspects. These Ethical Performance Indicators (EPI) allow adopting "appropriate measures of environmental [and social] protection in terms of effectiveness and efficiency; the empowerment of [..] [ethical] policy by a better definition and monitoring of [social and] environmental objectives; an effective definition of responsibilities and an aid for the implementation of [...] [an ethical] management systems; and the improvement of external and internal communication on [..] [sustainable] achievements and programs" (Bartolomeo, 1995).

As the definition indicates, EPIs have the potential to become a central management tool. This is further underlined by the establishment of ISO-Standards 14031 and 14032, defining Environmental Performance Evaluation as a "process to facilitate management decisions regarding an organization's environmental performance by selecting indicators, collecting and analysing data, assessing information against environmental performance criteria, reporting and communicating, and periodic review and improvement of this" (Gee, 2001, p. 26). Skilius and Wenneberg (1998, p. 6) added that EPIs prepare qualitative and quantitative ethical data in a more comprehensible way and help converting data into conclusive and concise information about social and environmental performance.

Yale University (2012, p. 16) has successfully established such indicators, but on country level.

2.2.3 Ethical Guiding Principles

Apart from environmental reports and EPIs, banks usually disclose their own Ethical Guiding Principles (EGP). However, reviewing internet-presentations and environmental reports of 28 banks standing for ethical behaviour (Appendix B), has resulted in major differences in the extent and content of EGPs. Given prior analysis of Environmental Reporting and EPIs, it is not surprising that there are large disagreements between the content, form and extent of bank's EGPs.

Especially local banks, like 'Femu qui' (Corsica) or 'Colonya Caixy Pollença' (Spain), disclose either no information on ethical principles or provide general information about corporate values, objectives or code of conducts. This is coherent with research by Melrose-Woodman and Kverndal (1976) - analysing ethical codes in 130 UK companies, showing that 60 companies did not disclose any ethical codes, following the opinion that "attitudes to social responsibility would be evident through management decisions" (Schlegelmilch & Houston, 1989, p. 10).

A different approach to implement ethics is an Ethical Policy Unit/Committee, as used by the 'Co-operative Bank' and 'Caisse Solidaire du Nord-Pas-de-Calais'. According to Winlow and Hall (2011, p. 400) such committees are an "attempt to compensate for the loss of the traditional symbolic order" and aim to ensure "that the bank has the appropriate means for promoting proper decision making and compliance with laws, regulations and internal rules; provides oversight of the compliance function" (Basel Committee on Banking Supervision, 2010, p. 13). Its tasks are similar to Sharia advisors in Islamic Banks because they help underlining the merits of Ethical Banking, establishing and monitoring the compliance with ethical principles, and informing customers. "In Islamic terms this is a matter of Ijtihad, [...] of fundamental principles to changing circumstances" (Wilson, 2002, p. 52). Hence, the committee should occupy a pro-active role - involved in business aspects and regulations.

Larger banks like the German 'GLS Bank', Dutch 'Triodos Bank' or British 'Unit Trust Bank' serve as pioneers and have sophisticated EGPs. Their ethical values are expressed in ethical codes and positive and negative criteria. This is in line with the idea of Islamic Banking, where banks conduct business according to Sharia principles, prohibiting Riba, Gharar and Maysir. Profit/Loss sharing and Halal activities are supported by Islamic Banks and serve as positive criteria. (Marimuthu, et al., 2010, pp. 53-54)

Wilson (2002, pp. 51-52) added a word of caution as "Islamic banks often describe themselves as [...] ethical financial services, but they do not spell out explicitly what is meant by this". However, one similarity between Ethical and Islamic Banks is that "the word ethical is used as a label, [...] but there is no attempt to make the link between what is ethical and the specific methods of conducting financial transactions [...] [and] to explain the ethical merits of how the bank conducts its business directly to the clients" (Wilson, 2002, pp. 51-52).

Hence, only few Ethical Banks disclose detailed information on their underlying ethical principles, commandments, prohibitions and their overall investment and lending policy. Merely stating to be ethical is insufficient.

2.3 Ethical decision making

Having discussed Ethical Bank's relevancy, the question arises what the term 'ethics' means and how it applies.

2.3.1 Definition

Although Ethical Banking is considered as a relatively new field of research, 'ethics' itself is not. According to Paliwal (2007, p. 3), over centuries philosophers struggled with approaches of humans towards ethics.

The term 'ethics' has its origin in ancient Greek. The word *ethikos* means customs, habit of life or tradition. When Cicero later searched for a Latin translation of the ancient Greek word, he chose *mos* ('moral'). Unless for some exceptions these two words have the same meaning (Grace & Cohen, 2010, p. 3 f.).

Ferrell, et al. (2010, p. 6) added that the term ethics has many nuances and "values and judgements generally play a critical role when we make ethical decisions". Reaching from Taylor's (1975, p. 1) "moral judgement, standards and rules of conduct", to the definition of The American Heritage Dictionary (2006, p. 611) as "the study of the general nature of morals and of the specific moral choices to be made by a person", to Wroe's (1965, p. 320) approach of differentiating ethical decisions from ordinary decisions or "the amount of emphasize that decision makers place on their own values and accepted practices within their company" (Ferrell, et al., 2010, p. 6).

According to Grace and Cohen (2010, p. 2) "ethical issues are often grey; [...] [and] people can differ on the subject of ethics as they may not on the laws of physics or the facts of geography". Crane and Matten (2010, p. 5) added that there are overlaps between law ("minimum acceptable standard of behaviour") and ethics, which they consider as the grey area. However, many moral issues are not covered by law.

In order to implement high ethical standards in society, individuals and companies need to follow moral principles. Collins (1994) argues that business ethics is an oxymoron because generally there can be no ethics in business and in a sense business itself is unethical (Crane & Matten, 2010, p. 4). Carr (1968) outlined that business, can be regarded as a game of poker, where different moral standards apply. Because of these divergences, it is inevitable to implement ethical rules and principles as company policy.

2.3.2 Theories

"In order to identify what makes acts right and wrong [...] we need to turn to major ethical theories" (Boatright, 2007, p. 31), which can enable us to think through ethical issues in business and make decisions.

Figure 6 provides a broad and simplified overview of theories. According to Fisher and Lovell (2009, p. 102), the horizontal dimensions are based on Dworkin's work on rights. Dworkin (1977, p. 22) defined 'policy' as "a goal to be reached, generally an improvement in some economic, political or social feature", whereas 'principle' was defined as a "standard that is to be observed, not because it will advance an economic, political or social situation, but because it is a requirement of fairness or justice or [...] morality" (Dworkin, 1977, p. 22). The vertical dimension (Figure 6) contrasts individual and institutional views on ethics, and the performance of their respective ethical duties towards society.

2.3.2.1 Teleology

According to Fisher and Lovell (2009, p. 125), "the rightness [...] of an action [...] can only be judged by its consequences". This means that the action is morally right, when it produces the desired result. Two teleological theories that guide decision-making are 'egoism' and 'utilitarianism'. With respect to banks, egoism-theory means that banks follow only their own personal interests, namely profit making, whereas utilitarianism-theory is based on continuous comparisons of costs and benefits to all stakeholders. (Ferrell,et al., 2010, p. 155)

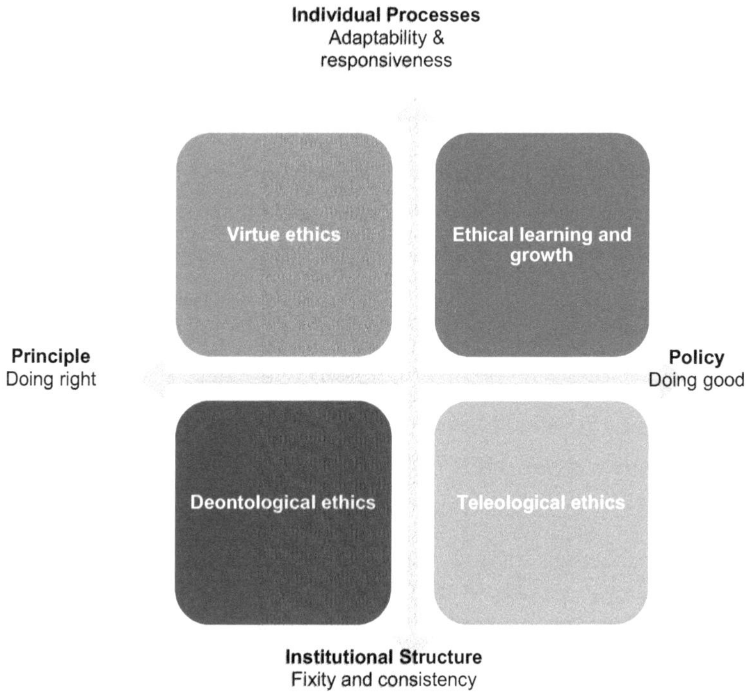

Figure 6: Framework for ethical theories (Fisher & Lovell, 2009, p. 102)

2.3.2.2 Deontology

Deontological ethics is a non-consequential theory based on duty. It has derived from religion as duties were written down in Thora's 613 Mitzvot or God's 10 biblical commandments. Its overall aim is fulfilling obligations based on the "principle of the matter" (Mizzoni, 2010, p. 104). At a later stage, Kant developed the religious approach to imperatives by defining duty as "something one is required to do" (Mizzoni, 2010, p. 177). Examples are the prohibition of torture, not to lie or not to break promises.

2.3.2.3 Virtue ethics

Virtue ethics are "personal qualities that provide the basis for the individual to lead a good, noble, or 'happy' life" (Fisher & Lovell, 2009, p. 103). Although virtue changed over time, the most recognised person on this subject stayed Aristotle who developed the idea of the 'great-soul-man', displaying virtues of the highest order within society. These virtues are personal characteristics that develop over time and help individuals make the right choices, but are not already present at birth (Aristotle & Ross, 2011, p. 13).

2.3.2.4 Ethical learning and growth

According to Fisher and Lovell (2009, p. 120 f.) ethical learning and growth theory is based on encouraging people to voluntary "learning that enable people to decide for themselves to act ethically".

This means that Ethical Banks have to specify EGPs, but the actual application and implementation must be carried out by each employee's actions. This is based on the idea that "policy [..] should be the yardstick against which the morality of actions should be judged, [...] [which] can only be achieved indirectly. An ethical organisation cannot be achieved by decree" (Fisher & Lovell, 2009, p. 120 f.). Famous theories are Individual Growth by Cowey and Senge, Communitarianism by Etzioni and Ethical Egoism by Rand (Fisher & Lovell, 2009, p. 120 f.).

2.3.3 Stakeholder Theory

Because the previous sub-chapter has given an introduction to ethical decision-making, the following will outline how a company can ensure ethical beliefs are reflected in their business.

To implement ethical beliefs, Goodpaster (1983), Campbell and Kitson (2008, p. 15) identified four steps a company has to carry out:

1. Identify issues and situations raising ethical questions,
2. Apply rational principles to produce ethical strategies and procedures,
3. Coordinate ethical strategies and procedures with demands, interests and constrains of stakeholders and
4. Implement agreed ethical strategies and procedures.

In the context of a fast-paced and ever-changing environment, banks have to continuously monitor and reassess their ethical strategies in order to guarantee adequate ethical behaviour (Meadowcroft, 2007, p. 156). Hence, a fifth stage should be added.

According to Ferrell, et al. (2010, p. 82) "to determine whether a specific [...] situation has an ethical component is to ask other individuals". This is consistent with stakeholder theory's core statement: "Paying attention to [...] stakeholders of a business is a useful way of developing ethically responsible behaviour" (Campbell & Kitson, 2008, p. 17). Therefore, stakeholder's opinion has to be included in determining Ethical Bank's EGPs.

2.4 Emerging issues and the need for empirical research

Because Ethical Banks have become serious competition for traditional banks, supposedly Ethical Banks and traditional banks use the term 'Ethical Bank' in order to sell bank services under the cloak of ethically correct conduct, although ethics is applied to individual products only or serves as a secondary objective. Therefore, standardised principles have to be introduced to build universally applicable rules Ethical Banks have to follow to be eligible to call themselves 'Ethical Bank'. This should be combined with the legal protection of the term 'Ethical Bank', so that violations against standards can be punished.

But because EGPs suffer from a "lack of agreement [...], it is difficult to find incidents of deviant behaviour which marketers would agree are [either ethical or] unethical" (Ferrell & Gresham, 1985, p. 87). Therefore empirical research has to be carried out to determine specific criteria either omitting or permitting Ethical Banks certain business. Stakeholder theory suggests that bank customers should be involved in this research, as "paying attention to [...] stakeholders [...] is a useful way of developing ethically responsible behaviour" (Campbell & Kitson, 2008, p. 17).

3 Theoretical Framework

According to Sevilla, et al. (2007, p. 55) a Theoretical Framework serves as an "interrelated construct [...] that presents a systematic view of phenomena by specifying relations among variables", aiming to present the linkage between literature and the attempted study.

The basis of this study is the triple-bottom-line concept, meaning that Ethical Banks engage in three key factors - social, environmental and economic development - while traditional banks focus on the latter one.

Because of bank's central role in the economy, they are required to satisfy specific prudential legal requirements for customer protection, supervised by committees in their respective countries, the European Banking Authority or Central Banks. Instruments like the protection of bank deposits, the Basel framework and national law imposing disclosure requirements, ensure safety of customer's money. Even during the crisis only few banks defaulted, rescue packages were put together quickly and banks at risk were taken over by other banks rather than defaulted (Gros & Mayer, 2010; Die Zeit Online, 2012). Because retail customer's deposits seem rather safe, the following study will investigate Ethical Bank's social and environmental aspects only.

As Literature Review results show, there are differences in defining Ethical Banks, in the way environmental and social data is disclosed and EGPs banks are applied. Because the disclosure is unstandardised, obscure and confusing for stakeholder, the identification of truly Ethical Banks is rarely possible for non-experts. Like law ensures security of bank deposits, ethically correct banks should be legally omitted or permitted to conduct certain business. According to Wilson (1997, p. 1326) this policy "can either be positive or negative, the former being supportive of companies which are particularly [ethically] approved [...]. The latter aims to avoid investing in companies which are involved in unacceptable products or countries, or whose business methods are regarded as unethical". In order to evaluate the ethicalness of decision and implement ethical belief into banks, the four-step model of Goodpaster (1983), Campbell and Kitson (2008, p. 15) shall be applied including Meadowcroft's (2007, p. 156) extension:

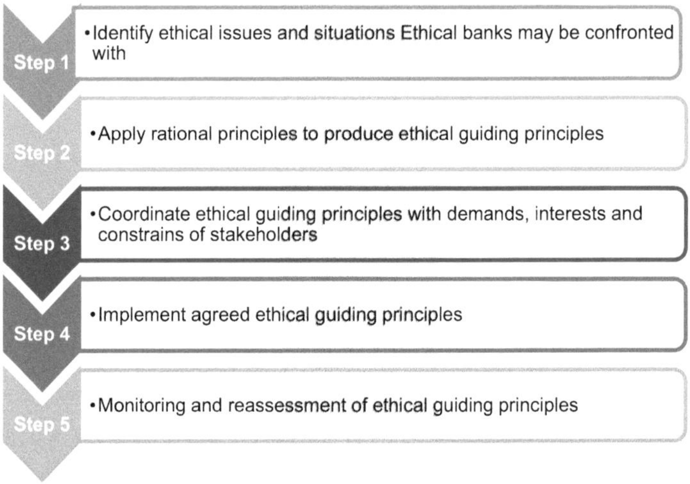

Figure 7: Four-step model to implement ethical beliefs

Within the research scope, step 1 will be carried out by content analysis of bank's environmental reports, homepage disclosures, guiding principles, investment and lending policies, as well as investment criteria used by EIRIS' ethical funds (Appendix B). The collected information serve as indicators for ethical issues banks may be confronted with.

In the second step, all collected information will be analysed, summarised and edited so that guiding principles can be derived from these information and ultimately categorised into groups.

In the third step, the categorised guiding principles will be coordinated with the demands, interest and constraints of stakeholders. Therefore, in accordance with stakeholder theory, stakeholders will be asked to express their opinion and experience with Ethical Banks and rate EGPs on a Likert's scale from 1 (ethical) to 5 (unethical). This is coherent with Literature Review findings, as "individuals [...] [have to be asked] how they feel about the ethicalness of a decision" (Ferrell, et al., 2010, p. 82) in order "to determine whether a specific behaviour or situation has an ethical component"(Ferrell, et al., 2010, p. 82).

After assessing the survey results, the identified positive and negative EGPs can be implemented. According to Burlando (2001, p. 377), the idea of establishing positive and negative EGPs goes back to the 1980s, when EIRIS established a catalogue of 'ethically negative' economic activities, later expanded by positive criteria (EIRIS, 2007). The problem is that these policies are rarely disclosed in detail and according to Wilson (1997, p. 1333) the adoption of an arbitrary 5% to 10% rule for unacceptable activities may be included. However, a percentage of unethical activities violates the ethical codex and ultimately betrays customer trust. Consequences must be the establishment of strict criteria and constant supervision of compliance.

The final step should be the continuous monitoring and reassessment of implemented principles because of the ever-changing environment.

4 Data and methodology

This chapter deals with research methodology and data collection. It includes a research design description and explanation of how the survey was established and conducted. Finally, practical problems and limitations will be discussed.

4.1 Research design

Polit and Hungler (1999, p. 155) defined research design as an outline for conducting studies so that control can be exercised over factors influencing the validity of the study's results. Research design is a plan to guide the study by obtaining answers to predetermined questions.

As the research onion by Saunders, et al. (2012, p. 128) shows (Figure 8), the researchers own beliefs and values can influence the research design and their respective results. Research approaches can differ from philosophical stances, practical considerations and important assumptions underpinning research strategy and methods chosen. Hence, the research approach is inevitably linked to the research question, aims and objectives of the study.

4.1.1 Post-positivism

This study follows a post-positivist approach, but allows research outcomes to be interpretative and explanatory. According to Robson (2002, p. 18), positivism requires research to be "carried out systematically, sceptically and ethically", focussing on data collection and facts. The positivist belief in empirical testability is broadly associated with quantitative research. Hence, well-structured empirical research based on numerical data is required to prove literature concepts and theories. The objective view, which is closely connected to positivism, accepts observable and measurable facts as empirically verifiable (Crotty, 1998, p. 27; Hart, 2005, p. 409). Crotty (1998, p. 27) argued further that the objective view aims to detect universal realities based on "objective, empirically verifiable" knowledge.

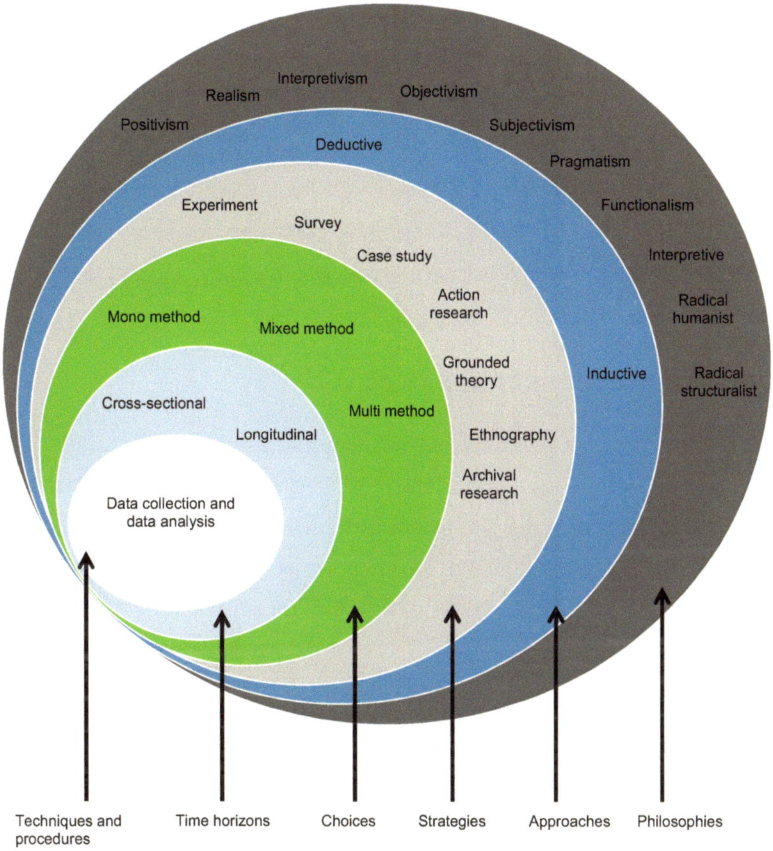

Figure 8: Saunders' (2012, p. 128) research onion model

This research suggests that individuals and banks have different opinions on ethical and unethical behaviour. This does not comply with objectivism but embraces an interpretivist scientific thought. From an interpretivist viewpoint, "meanings are constructed by human beings as they engage with the world they are interpreting" (Crotty, 1998, p. 43). Hence, interactions between individuals in society and interactions with the environment may construct meanings, realities and notions that differ and bear "quite different connotations" (Crotty, 1998, p. 43).

To ground this research's logic, empirical research based on numerical data needs to be approached from a subjective epistemological viewpoint – the post-positivist theoretical perspective. The post-positivist philosophical stance rejects the positivist view of "the objective existence of meaningful reality" (Crotty, 1998, p. 40), but adopts a more constructionist viewpoint by allowing research outcomes to be interpretive and explanatory (Ryan, 2006, p. 18).

Because this study embraces a post-positivist stance, research aims are more of a "learning role rather than a testing one" (Ryan, 2006, p. 18). Based on numerical data, this research explores bank customers' banking habits and ethical views, notions and opinions towards sustainability and categories of EGPs.

4.1.2 Inductive research approach

Emerging from different philosophical assumptions, Saunders, et al. (2012, p. 143 ff.) offered two research approaches – deductive and inductive. While the deductive approach focuses on empirical hypothesis testing, the inductive approach aims to explore a field by reviewing existing concepts and theories. David and Sutton (2011, p. 108 ff.) added that it is a widely held belief that deductive research is quantitative, whereas inductive research is qualitative. However, the blurring of this distinction is common in this context.

As this research is not meant to be hypothetically tested, it offers guidelines for implementing EGPs into Ethical Banks. This is consistent with the viewpoint that "theory should be built up from exploration of reality, not used to predict it" (David & Sutton, 2011, p. 14), making this research an inductive approach.

4.2 Survey

This sub-chapter aims to describe the research process by explaining the research design, applied survey method and distribution.

4.2.1 Research process

The actual fieldwork of the research process consists of four stages:

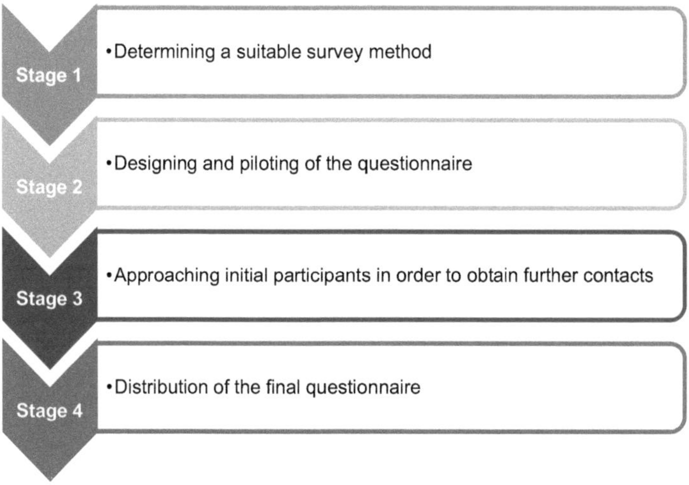

Figure 9: Research process

In the first stage, a suitable research method was chosen to meet the research aim and purpose. Because the overall aim of this study is to identify EGPs stakeholders agree on, the method of snowball-sampling was chosen.

The second stage of the research process consisted of designing and piloting the questionnaire. After relevant questions were established - based on bank's environmental reports, homepage disclosures, existing guiding principles, investment and lending policies of EIRIS' investment funds (Appendix B) - a logical sequence was determined and a pilot survey established. Amendments by the responsible research supervisor were proposed and implemented, before conducting the pilot study.

According to Blessing and Chakrabarti (2009, p. 114), a pilot study can detect potential problems and negative factors influencing the quality and validity of the results. It is basically a trial base survey, so that problems are revealed, improved or prevented before the final questionnaire is carried out. To ensure comprehensibility of the research question, the pilot study was carried out on 5 participants. Results show that participants had completely understood the questions, but the evaluation scale of criteria had to be revised. Chapter 4.2.1.2 deals with survey design in more detail.

Simultaneously, the third stage was carried out, compromising the acquisition of further participants on basis of snowball-sampling. Sub-chapter 4.2.1.1 will provide further details.

After having revised the questionnaire and obtained further participants with the help of snowball-sampling, the last stage was executed – the distribution of the final questionnaire to all participants.

4.2.1.1 Survey method and distribution

This research follows a quantitative approach using an online questionnaire created with GoogleDocs to collect primary data. The advantage of GoogleDocs is that it is free of charges, has the ability to create unlimited questions, is technically simple, easy to include a logical sequence into the questions and is straightforward in exporting the data to Excel and eViews (Google, 2012).

An online-survey was chosen because it is a fast and cheap way to interview participants in several countries over a time period at any time of the day. Furthermore it ensures privacy and anonymity, which may ultimately promote authentic answers. (Denscombe, 2010, p. 178; Bethlehem & Biffignandi, 2012, p. 46 ff; Russell & Purcell, 2009, p. 27 ff)

With respect to the explanatory research purpose, the nonprobability snowball-sampling method was used. According to Babbie (2010, p. 193f.), snowball-sampling is a process where "each located subject suggests other subjects". It is primarily used for exploratory studies and an informal method to access a wide population (David & Sutton, 2011, p. 232).

The online-survey was sent to 100 EEA bank customers within the researcher's social network. Further potential customers were contacted, so that ultimately 243 stakeholders were invited and 96 responded (chapter 5.1).

According to David and Sutton (2011, p. 232), snowball-sampling is often criticised for inevitably resulting in biased samples, as the researcher relies on his social contacts to invite survey participants. However, the advantage is that extensive data can be gathered because the sample size can grow considerably with this technique.

4.2.1.2 Survey design

The survey consists of 26 questions (see Appendix A). Most of them are closed-ended questions that limit participants' answers to a fixed set of responses. Closed-end responses are easier to evaluate, as they can often be directly transferred into an Excel-format. However, if the researcher did not properly structure responses, they may be left unanswered. In order to overcome such issues, open-ended questions were added which allow individual answers. (Babbie, 2010, p. 255).

Types of closed-end questions used in the questionnaire are either multiple-choice questions or Likert's scales offering the following five answer possibilities to measure participants' attitude towards certain business situations (Albert & Tullis, 2008, p. 124):

1) Agree strongly that this criterion is ethical;
2) Agree to some extend that this criterion is ethical;
3) Undecided whether the criterion is ethical or not;
4) This criterion being ethical applies to a lesser extend;
5) This criterion being ethical does not apply at all.

Although survey research has its disadvantages, it allows establishing a panoramic, but limited and therefore accessible framework to investigate the concepts discussed in the Literature Review.

The questions addressed bank customer's attitude towards sustainability and ethics in general, their banking habits and ethical attitude towards the following nine areas:

- Leisure and entertainment,
- Animals and plants,
- Weapons,
- Energy,
- Medical and pharmaceuticals,
- Commodities,
- Transportation,
- Law, International Agreements and Corporate Governance,
- Finance and Support.

4.3 Data collection and analysis

The collected data included nominal, continuous and ordinal variables. The quantitative variables were coded and analysed using eViews.

Having created the questionnaire using GoogleDocs, the data is already preformatted as a spreadsheet and can be transformed into an Excel or eViews file. Because this research aims to answer the question which business transactions are either preferred or omitted for Ethical Banks according to bank customer's judgement, the questionnaire's key areas were nine predetermined business areas (chapter 4.2.1.2).

To evaluate each criterion's ethical relevancy (positive criteria), respectively filter out unethical conduct (negative criteria), number one ("Agree strongly that this criterion can be considered ethical") and two ("Agree to some extend that this criterion can be considered ethical") of Likert's scale were summed up, as well as number four ("This criterion being ethical applies to a lesser extend") and five ("This criterion being ethical does not apply at all").

After having added the gradations, the results were benchmarked against 50%. This means that if 50% of the participants agreed on one criterion being either strongly ethical or to some extend ethical, this particular criterion was added to the final list of positive criteria, which shall ultimately set the standard for Ethical Banks being present in the EEA. Negative criteria vice versa.

The benchmark of 50% was chosen because - as absolute majority - this "rule is a time-honoured, simple and egalitarian way of aggregating individual preferences" (Chapman, 1990, p. 73). In this case the majority of survey participants should decide what is considered as being ethical or unethical behaviour. The special role of the 'absolute majority' rule becomes further evident when looking at politics or shareholder voting.

4.4 Practical research problems

Saunders, et al. (2012, p. 208) acknowledge access as being a "critical aspect for the success of any research project". EEAs bank customers represent the population, which enables this project to access a high number of individuals. However, only 96 individuals out of 243 answered the questionnaire.

62 responses were collected after distributing the survey for the first time. After sending a reminder-email two weeks later, 96 responses were generated in total. The low response rate (39.5%) may be connected to the length of the survey - 26 questions with up to 36 items. This may inhibit participant's willingness to complete the questions. Furthermore, survey content requiring participants to answer personal questions about pornographic, legal or financial content may inhibit the willingness further. But because survey-questions are connected to the results of the Literature Review, the large scope of the empirical study was necessary.

Further errors may arise due to language barriers and lack of technical knowledge or equipment, making it impossible to understand or fill out the questionnaire. Although "English is the most widely understood [language]" (European Commission, 2012b) in Europe, some of the questions contain technical terms that can falsify the results because of comprehensibility issues.

5 Findings and analysis of results

The study aims to quantitatively examine individuals' attitude towards Ethical Banking and their personal opinions on concrete examples of business situations. In the following, the findings of quantitative research will be discussed with reference to the concepts outlined in the Literature Review.

5.1 Respondents' characteristics and attitude towards different bank types

As Figure 10 shows, the majority of participants resides in the UK and Germany. Due to the fact that the researcher himself commutes between Germany and the UK; and the selection of interviewees was by personal E-Mail-invitation, it is comprehensible that the concrete choice of participants was influences by the researcher's preferences and circle of acquaintances. This is consistent with Saunders, et al. (2012, p. 128) (chapter 4.1).

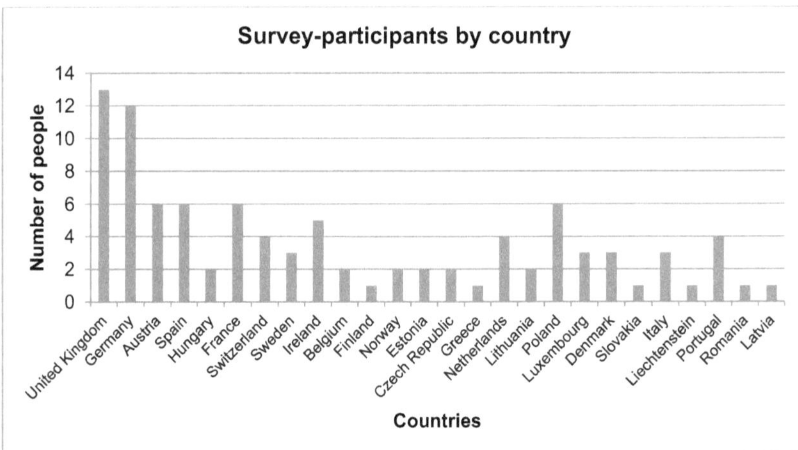

Figure 10: Survey-participants by country

The gender is distributed evenly among the participants (55.2% female, 44.8% male), the absolute majority being within the age rage of 20 to 40 years, accounting for 58.3%, followed by 0 to 20 years old (16%). This is due to the survey being conducted online and these age ranges being referred to as "The Net Generation" (Tapscott, 2009) with an innate understanding of technology.

With respect to awareness levels of social and environmental issues, 77.08% consider themselves as either being absolutely aware or possess the ability to recognise environmental and social issues. Only 5.21% of the respondents care neither about the environment nor other people around them.

Findings reveal that 78.1% of the respondents have their bank products (on average respondents owns 3.9 bank products) either at one primary bank (37.5%) or spread between two banks (40.6%). However, research shows that 85.4% are not happy with their primary bank and planning on changing it soon, which is in line with the finding of Ernst & Young (2011, p. 7) (chapter 1.1). Reasons are primarily unsatisfactory service standards and prices, the distance to the branch or even the banks secrecy standards.

Because of the high dissatisfaction among customers, the next questions will concentrate on Ethical Banks, serving as an alternative to traditional banks.

Findings outline that 43.75% of the participants have heard of the term Ethical Bank and are aware of the fact that there are differences between banks solely offering ethical products or following a completely ethical business approach. 19.05% even having an account with a presumably Ethical Bank, namely GLS Bank, Crédal, Cultura Sparebank, ETIKA, Valartis Bank, TISE, Ethik Bank and HSBC.

5.2 Evaluation of ethical criteria

As the Literature Review indicates, Ethical Banks can be defined by the business they conduct. On the one hand - to be ethical - they need to refrain (negative criteria) from conducting their business in certain fields of business that in the broadest sense compromises unethical behaviour. On the other hand, they need to support as many ethical projects (positive criteria) as possible.

As already outlined in chapter 4.3, an approval rate of more than 50% will either determine criteria as being ethical or unethical. Criteria below 50% do not possess the necessary relevancy to make it to the final criteria list.

The following nine sub-chapters are divided according to different business challenges Ethical Banks may be exposed to - summarised according to the participant's ethical perception of being either positive or negative. A theoretical approach to explain ethical decision-making by individuals was outlined in chapter 2.3.2.

5.2.1 Leisure and entertainment

Following the concept of an absolute majority, participants consider pornography and gambling as ethically incorrect (see Figure 11), however not alcohol and tobacco.

This may be due to the participation of smokers in the questionnaire and those enjoying responsible consumption of alcohol in the free time. Contributing to these results may be that the majority of participants are in the age range of 0 to 40. As studies by McDermott, et al. (2006) and Clapp, et al. (2006) have shown, this age range shows a statistically higher rate for smoking and drinking alcohol. Coffee-Shops are not considered ethically incorrect either, as they are legally approved in the Netherlands.

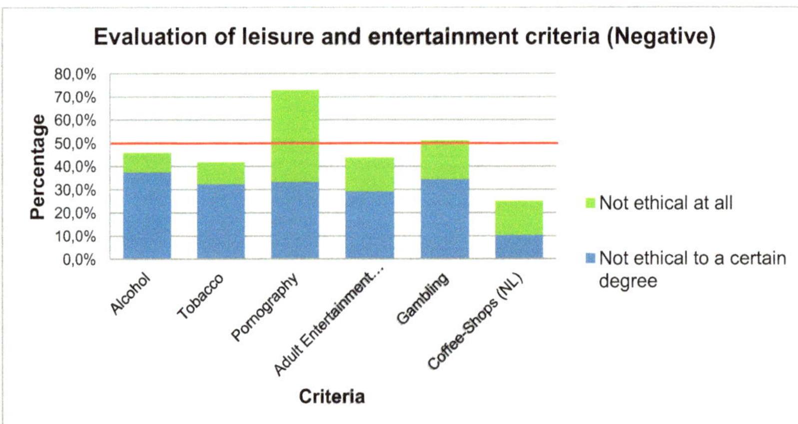

Figure 11: Evaluation of negative leisure and entertainment criteria

Figure 12 gives information about positive ethical leisure and entertainment criteria. Because the approval rate of ethically correct business transactions is 50%, none of the criteria comes past this rate. Surprisingly only Coffee-Shops manage to come close to the 50% benchmark.

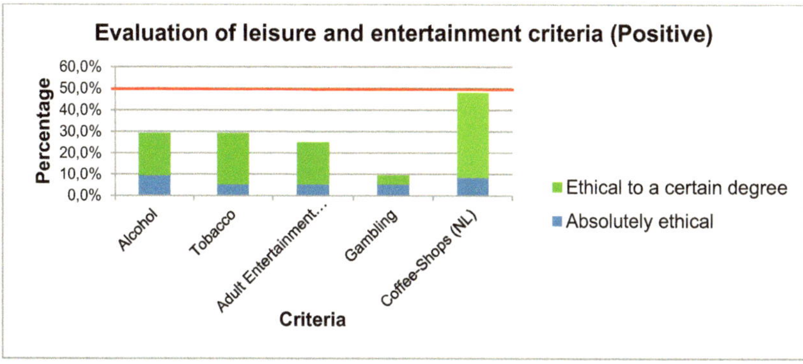

Figure 12: Evaluation of positive leisure and entertainment criteria

5.2.2 Animals and plants

Figure 13 shows that animal testing and fur trade are considered unethical. With 49%, the industry of animal disposal is close to the benchmark followed by intensive farming with 31.25% - however, both have not reached 50% yet. Figures may change in the future as they are subject to trends and personal assessment.

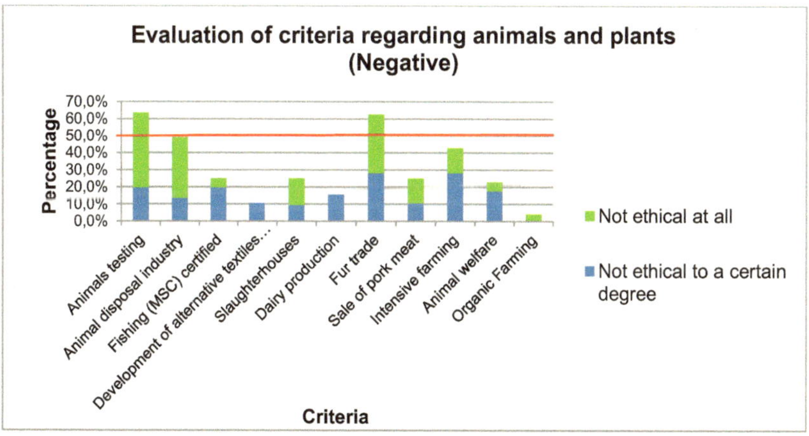

Figure 13: Evaluation of negative animal and plant criteria

More meaningful than the results of negative criteria, are (Figure 14) positive criteria.

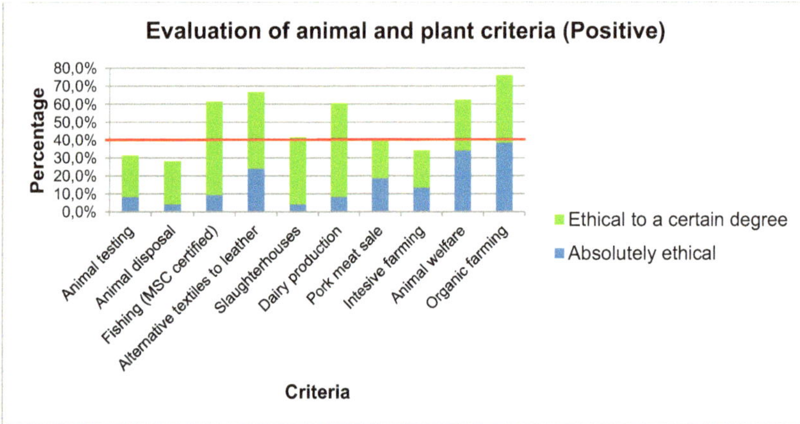

Figure 14: Evaluation of positive animal and plant criteria

Organic farming, the development of alternative textiles to leather, animal welfare, MCS certified fishing and dairy production are considered ethical. These results are not unexpected, more surprising is the fact that slaughterhouses and animal testing receive such high agreement to being ethical.

5.2.3 Weapons

Survey results show very unambiguous results because all types of weapons were rejected except for paintball activities and sport shooting (Figure 15). Both - sport shooting and paintball – have no intention to kill anybody and are exclusively for fun. Paintball activities require food colour cartridges and sport shooting (not to be confused with sport hunting) does not feature any living targets.

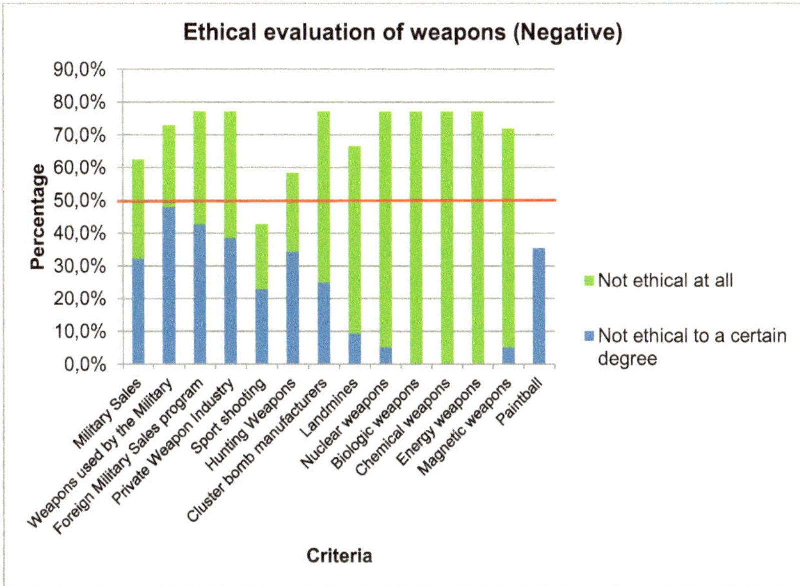

Figure 15: Evaluation of negative weapon criteria

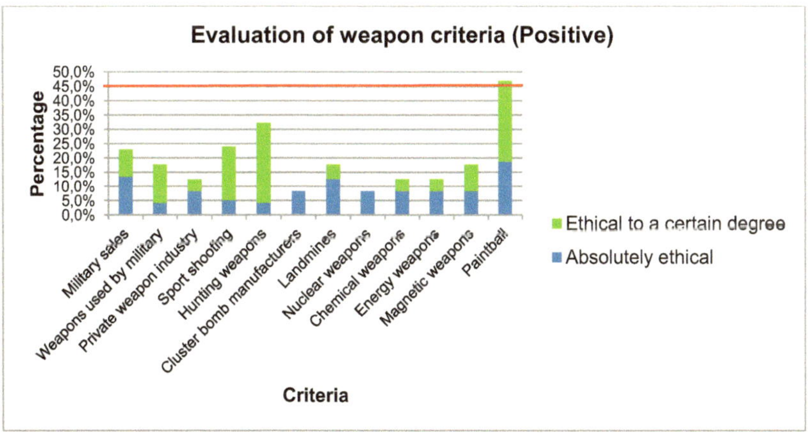

Figure 16: Evaluation of positive weapon criteria

Figure 16 displays none of the weapons as being ethically correct. Only paintball has the potential to reach the benchmark. Nevertheless, surprising is the broad consent on hunting weapons (32.3%), as they were declined being ethical in the previous figure.

5.2.4 Energy

The results for negative energy criteria are bewildering as renewable energy sources like geothermal energy and waste incineration plants are considered unethical. This may be the case for old waste incineration plants, as they created "toxic effluents, gases and chemicals, which [..] endanger[ed] the groundwater" (Endress, 2012), but with new standards (European Parliament , 2000) "this danger can be avoided and the energy created in the burning process can be captured and re-used" (Endress, 2012). Geothermal energy however is energy obtained from the earth's internal heat and satisfies all requirements for being ethical.

44.8% even considered recycling to be unethical. Either interviewees lacked understanding and fundamental knowledge of energy concepts or language barriers prevented participants to answer the survey questions truthfully.

Because of those contradictory results, negative energy criteria are not added to the final list as the results make logically no sense.

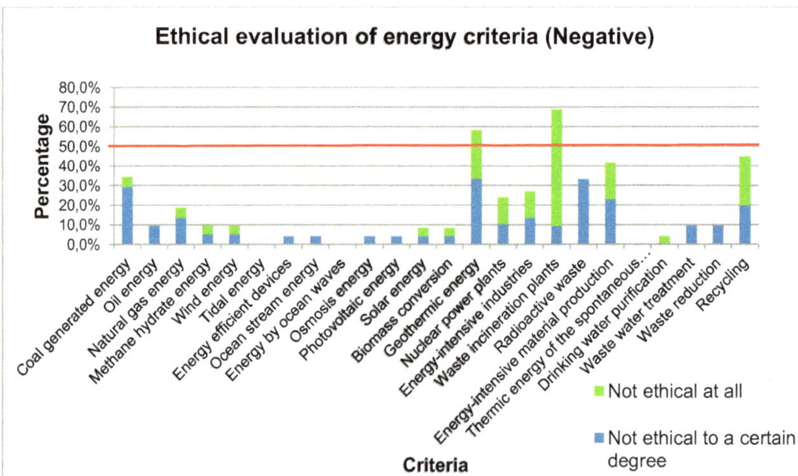

Figure 17: Evaluation of negative energy criteria

In contrast to negative energy criteria, participants were very well capable of determining positive energy power sources (Figure 18). Unambiguous results show that renewable energy projects are preferred in comparison to traditional energy sources like oil or coal energy. Hence, positive criteria can be added to the final list of positive criteria.

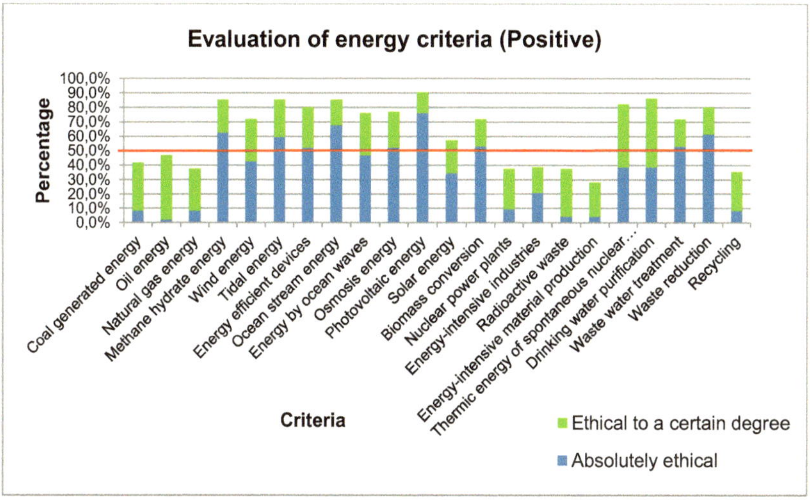

Figure 18: Evaluation of positive energy criteria

5.2.5 Medical and pharmaceuticals

In Figure 19 it is striking that only companies with health and safety offenses are regarded as unethical, whereas controversial topics such as embryonic stem cell research, xenotransplantation or life termination services are either appraised as not clearly unethical or even ethical (Figure 20). Reasons for considering life termination services (e.g. assisted suicide or abortion) to be ethically correct may originate from assisted suicide being legal in several EEA countries, such as the Netherlands and Switzerland. But, although abortions are generally allowed in the EEA (2.7% abortion rate), Malta and Andorra still consider it to be illegal on any grounds (World Health Organization, 2012; Guttmacher Institute, 2012).

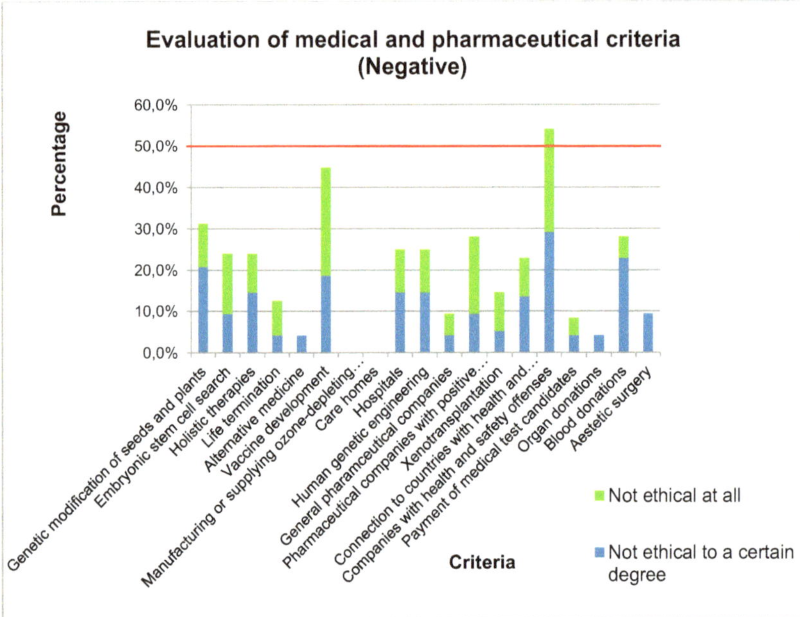

Figure 19: Evaluation of negative medical and pharmaceutical criteria

Another self-contradictory positive criterion is the manufacture of supplying ozone-depleting chemicals. Because ozone-depleting chemicals have a negative impact on our environment, this criterion does not meet the requirements of the World Commission on Environmental and Development (1987, p. 41) (chapter 2.1.1), hence must be deleted from the final list of positive guiding principles.

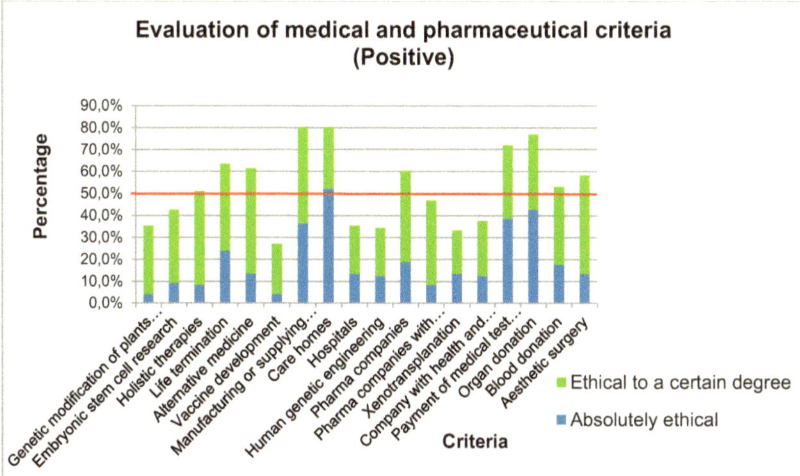

Figure 20: Evaluation of positive medical and pharmaceutical criteria

5.2.6 Commodities

Surprisingly, only conventional agriculture is pursued as being ethically incorrect (Figure 21).

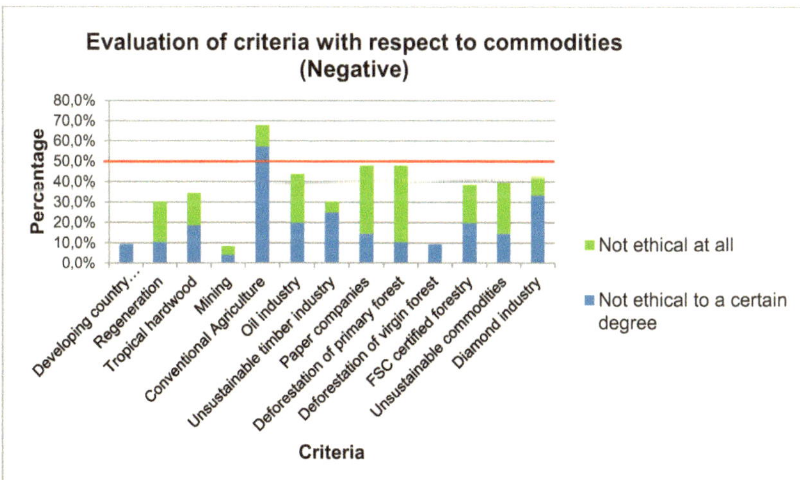

Figure 21: Evaluation of negative commodity criteria

Positive criteria (Figure 22) however compromise commodities from developing countries, mining, unsustainable timber industry and deforestation of virgin forest.

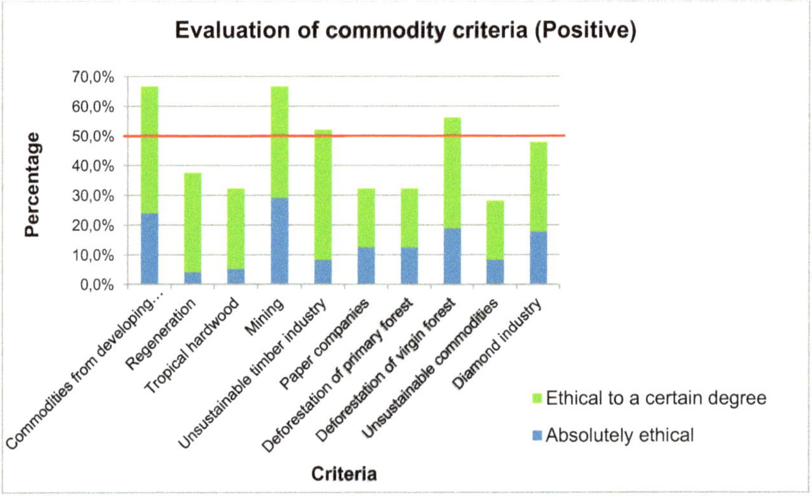

Figure 22: Evaluation of positive commodity criteria

52.1%, respectively 56.3% of the participants considered the unsustainable timber industry and deforestation of virgin forest to be ethically correct. Again, interviewees lacked understanding, fundamental knowledge or language barriers to answer the survey questions truthfully. Because of contradictory results, unsustainable timber industry and deforestation of virgin forest cannot be added to the final list as the results make logically no sense and ultimately damage the nature.

5.2.7 Transportation

As previous results have shown, making decisions about criteria can be difficult and opinions can be widely spread. Especially the determination of negative criteria seems to be a problem for the survey participants, whereas it seems easier to agree on positive criteria. Therefore it is not surprising that, again only one negative criterion was determined by the majority of participants (Figure 23) - the air travel industry.

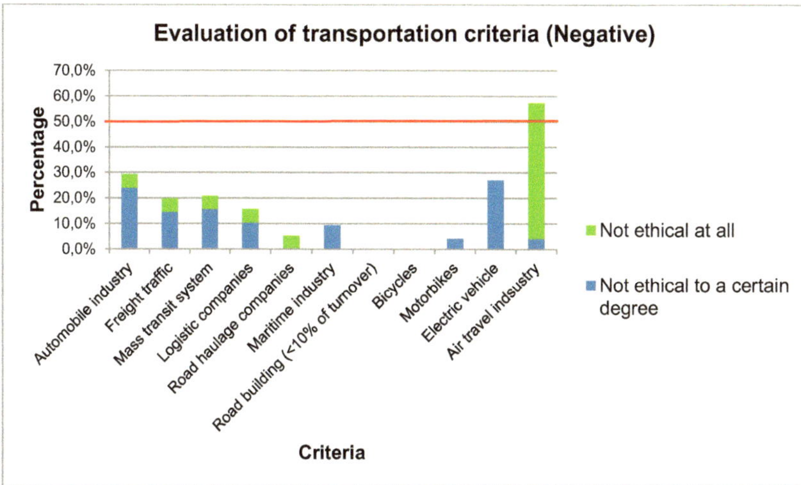

Figure 23: Evaluation of negative transportation criteria

Figure 24 shows that six out of eleven predetermined criteria are deemed to be ethical. The eligible criteria will be added to the final list of positive criteria.

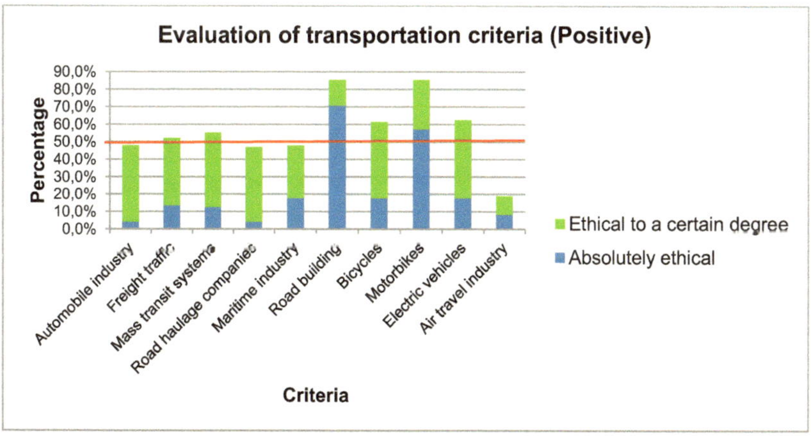

Figure 24: Evaluation of positive transportation criteria

5.2.8 Law, International Agreements, Corporate Governance

Compliance with environmental policies and the violation of Civil rights are considered to be unethical (Figure 25). Again, an originally positive criterion (compliance with environmental policies) is regarded as negative.

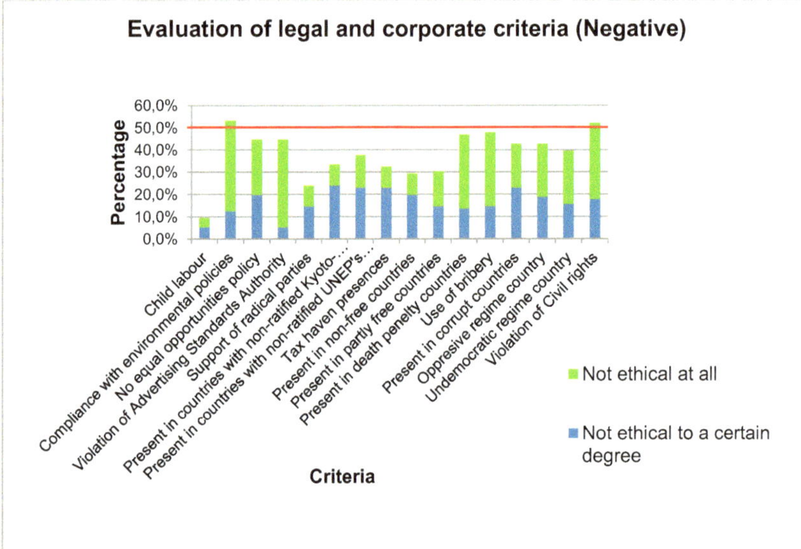

Figure 25: Evaluation of negative legal and corporate criteria

A similar phenomenon - with an originally negative criteria being regarded as positive - is shown in Figure 26, as child labour and convictions of serious pollution are considered to be positive.

According to UNICEF “child labour [...] damage[s] children’s health, threaten[s] their education and lead[s] to further exploitation and abuse” (2007, p. 52). Therefore, neither child labour nor projects that support convictions of serious pollution can be regarded as ethically correct and must be deleted from the final list.

Given that absurd results occur concentrated towards the end of the survey, the length of the survey may be to blame for, as the power of concentration and internal motivation decreases. Both factors may inhibit participant’s willingness to complete the questions conscientiously and carefully.

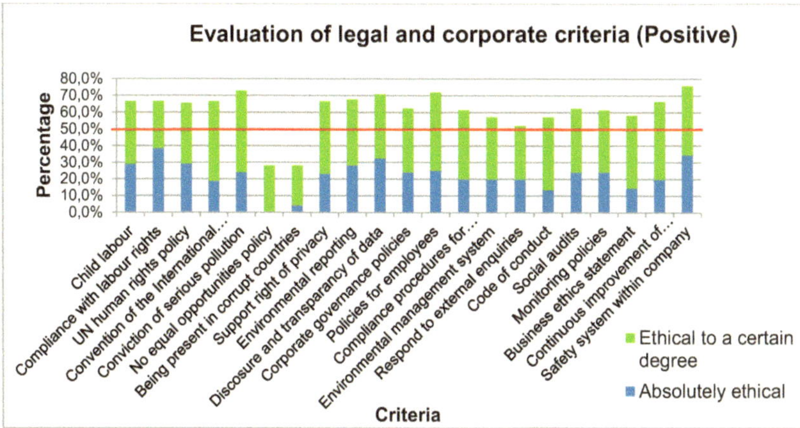

Figure 26: Evaluation of positive legal and corporate criteria

5.2.9 Finance and Support

Figure 27 illustrates negative financial and social criteria. None of the criteria were estimated as unethical.

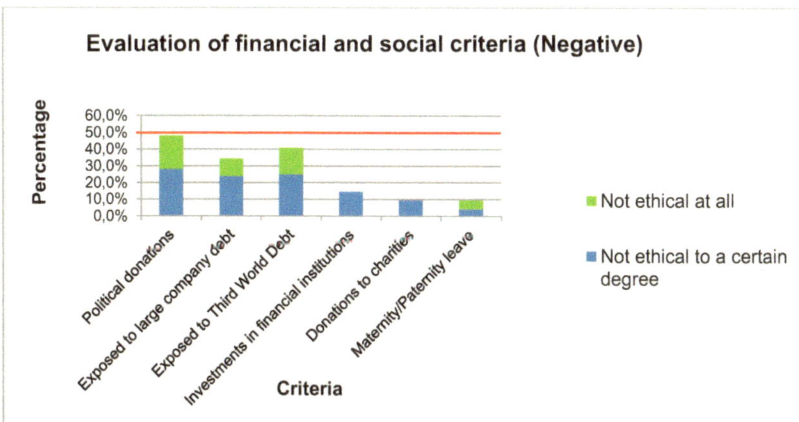

Figure 27: Evaluation of negative financial and social criteria

Figure 28 shows selected positive financial and social criteria. For both positive and negative criteria it is striking that results make logically sense, although it is the last question of the survey to answer. This may be due to the fact that there is no specialised knowledge required in order to find the matching appraisal on Likert's scale.

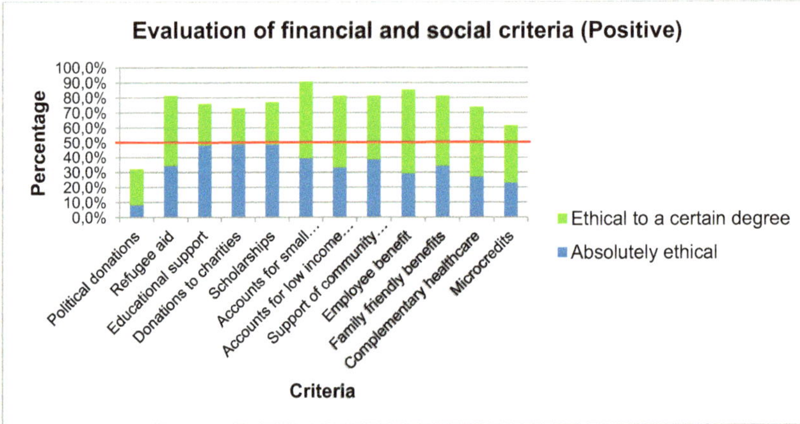

Figure 28: Evaluation of positive financial and social criteria

5.3 Final list of criteria

The following tables summarise the survey findings, categorised according to negative and positive criteria.

Positive criteria serve as suggestions for investment and lending opportunities and negative criteria strictly forbid any business, either directly or indirectly through third parties.

Positive criteria	
MSC certified Fishing	Bicycles
Alternative textiles to leather	Motorbikes
Dairy production	Electric vehicles
Animal welfare	Compliance with labour rights
Organic farming	UN human rights policy
Methane hydrate energy	Convention of the International Labour Organisation
Wind energy	Support right of privacy
Tidal energy	Environmental reporting
Energy efficient devices	Disclosure and transparency of data
Ocean stream energy	Sound corporate governance policies
Energy by ocean waves	Policies for employees
Osmosis energy	Compliance procedures for employees
Photovoltaic energy	Environmental management system
Solar energy	Respond fully to external enquiries
Biomass conversion	Code of conduct available
Thermic energy of spontaneous nuclear disintegration	Social audits
Drinking water purification	Monitoring of policies

Positive criteria	
Waste water treatment	Business ethics statement
Waste reduction	Continuous improvement of sustainable activities
Life termination	Safety system within the company
Alternative medicine	Refugee aid
Pharmaceutical companies in general	Educational support
Payment of medical test candidates	Donations to charities
Organ donation	Scholarships
Blood donation	Accounts for small businesses
Aesthetic surgery	Accounts for low income customers
Commodities from developing countries	Support of community
Mining	Employee benefit
Freight traffic	Family friendly benefits
Mass transit systems	Complementary healthcare
Road building	Microcredits
Waste water treatment	Business ethics statement
Waste reduction	Continuous improvement of sustainable activities
Life termination	Safety system within the company

Table 1: Final list of positive criteria

Negative Criteria	
Pornography	Biological weapons
Gambling	Chemical weapons
Animal testing	Energy weapons
Fur trade	Magnetic weapons
Military sales of weapon	Connection to countries with health and safety offenses
Weapons used by the military	Conventional agriculture
Foreign Military Sales program	Air travel industry
Private Weapon industry	Compliance with environmental policies
Hunting Weapons	Violation of Civil rights
Cluster bomb manufacturers	Nuclear weapons
Landmines	

Table 2: Final list of negative criteria

6 Conclusion

The overall aim of this research was to make truly Ethical Banks distinguishable from other types of banks by investigating, analysing and determining principles, Ethical Banks have to fulfil or refrain from in order to call themselves ethical. This following chapter will revisit the research objective above by summarising findings and limitations, and provide an outline for further research.

6.1 Summary of findings

As the Literature Review has shown, there are several approaches to define Ethical Banks, but not one uniform definition. Hence, banks use the term 'Ethical Bank' to sell bank services under the cloak of ethical business conduct, although they have not reached Jeucken's sustainability stage (Figure 3). Especially because of bank's critical intermediary role, standards need to be set to guarantee bank's ethical behaviour, offer certainty for customers and simplify their search for an Ethical Bank.

As an analysis of approaches to disclose, measure and set standards of ethical behaviour has shown, the best applicable method is the introduction of EGPs. Therefore, quantitative research, in accordance with ethical and stakeholder theory, has focused on determining positive and negative EGPs.

Survey results have confirmed that participants are not in agreement of what is ethical or unethical. Furthermore, it was observed that it was easier for participants to choose positive criteria (62 criteria), than to determine what is negative (21 criteria). Another issue was that in some cases results were illogical. Illogical criteria were not incorporated in the final criteria list.

6.2 Limitations

Apart from limitations one has to bear in mind when interpreting the online-questionnaire results (chapter 4.4.), an issue surrounding this study is the continuously changing environment, making the determination of criteria difficult. What is correct today can be overtaken tomorrow. Hence, as outlined in the Theoretical Framework, continuous reviewing and validation of criteria is necessary. For the time being however, the results can be considered as up to date and may serve as basis for further research.

If criteria were implemented as Ethical Bank standards, it would be necessary to establish a control mechanism within or outside the bank that monitors compliance with EGPs such as a Sharia Supervisory Board would do to Islamic Banks by making sure the banks operations do not involve “any element that is prohibited” (Institute of Islamic Banking and Insurance, 2012).(Lee & Yang, 2000, p. 791)

6.3 Opportunities for further research

One research obstacle (chapter 2.2.2) is that metrics are missing in this study in order to measure or target ethical behaviour. But because the definition of metrics is dependent on the underlying guiding principle, the initial step must be defining EGPs to determine concrete metrics in the next step. Hence setting metrics may serve as a possible future research area.

With respect to further investigations, an interesting topic to research is the personal motivation behind survey answers. Building on these survey results, the same participants could be interviewed again (e.g. in a face-to-face interview), but this time focussing on the selection of criteria and their motivation behind each choice. For instance to investigate if smokers were more likely to consider smoking as ethically correct and non-smokers as ethically incorrect.

VI References

Al-Ajmi, J., Al-Saleh, N., & Abo Hussain, A. (2011). Investment appraisal practices: A comparative study of conventional and Islamic financial institutions. *Advances in Accounting, incorporating Advances in International Accounting* (27), 111-124.

Albert, W., & Tullis, T. (2008). *Measuring the user experience.* Burlington: Elsevier.

Aristotle, & Ross, D. W. (2011). *Nicomachean Ethics.* Seattle: Pacific Publishing Studio.

Arsov, A. (2008). *Strategic sustainability of investment and business: Case of Commercial Bank Belgrade.* Grenoble Graduate School of Business, Grenoble.

Babbie, E. (2010). *The Practice of Social Research* (Vol. 12). Belmont: Cengage Learning.

Barbu, T. C., & Boitan, I. A. (2009). The financial crisis impacts on ethical financial institutions. *Annals of Faculty of Economics* (1), 467-473.

Bartolomeo, M. (1995). Environmental performance indicators in industry. *Nota di Lavoro* , 41-95.

Basel Committee on Banking Supervision. (2010). *Principles for enhancing corporate governance.* Basel: Bank for International Settlements.

Bernanke, B. S. (1983). Nonmonetary Effects on the Financial Crisis In the Propagation of the Great Depression. *The Amercan Economic Review* (3), 257-276.

Bethlehem, J., & Biffignandi, S. (2012). *Handbook of Web Surveys.* Hoboken: John Wiley & Sons.

Blessing, L. T., & Chakrabarti, A. (2009). *DRM, a Design Research Methodolgy.* London: Springer-Verlag.

Bloomberg. (2011, December 11). *European Banks Fail To Back Enough Green Projects, UNEP FI Says*. Retrieved July 27, 2012 from http://www.bloomberg.com/news/2011-12-07/european-banks-fail-to-back-enough-green-projects-unep-fi-says.html

Boatright, J. R. (2007). *Ethics and the Conduct of Business* (Vol. 5). New Jersey: Pearson Prentice Hall.

Boatright, J. R. (2008). *Ethics in Finance* (2nd ed.). Oxford: Blackwell Publishing.

Bosshard, P. (1998, November). *Ilisu - A Test Case of International Policy Coherence.* (B. Declaration, Ed.) Retrieved September 26, 2012 from RiverNet - The Ilisu dam project: http://www.rivernet.org/turquie/ilisu.htm#Introduction

Bouma, J. J., Jeucken, M., & Klinkers, L. (2001). *Sustainable Banking: The Greening of Finance.* Sheffield, UK: Greenleaf Publishing.

Boyer, M., & Laffont, J.-J. (1997). Environmental risks and bank liability. *European Economic Review , 41*, 1427-1459.

Bryman, A., & Bell, E. (2007). *Business Research Methods* (Vol. 2). Oxford: Oxford University Press.

Bundesministerim der Justiz. (2012, October 1). *KWG §1.* Retrieved October 1, 2012 from Translated from German by H. Heerdt: http://www.gesetze-im-internet.de/kredwg/__1.html

Burkhardt, A., Franzen, O., & Kumbartzki, J. (2005). Markenbewertung für Corporate Brands. *Planung & Analyse* (3), 1-13.

Burlando, R. M. (2001). Ethical finance: Its achievements in Great Britain and Italy. *World Futures: The Journal of Global Education , 56* (4), 369-398.

Burns, N., & Grove, S. (1997). *The practice of nursing research* (Vol. 3). Philadelphia: Saunders.

Cabaleiro Casal, J., & Rodríguez Parada, S. M. (2007). Sociedades cooperativas de banca alternativa. *Ekonomiaz* (65), 228-259.

Campbell, R., & Kitson, A. (2008). *The ethical organisation* (Vol. 2). London: Palgrave MacMillan.

Canadian Institute of Chartered Accountants. (1994). *Reporting on Environmental Performance.* Toronto: CICA.

Carr, A. (1968). Is Business Bluffing Ethical? *Harvard Business Review , 46*, 143-153.

Chapman, J. (1990). *School-based decision-making and management.* Basingstoke: The Falmer Press.

Clapp, J. D., Reed, M. B., Holmes, M. R., Lange, E., & Voas, R. B. (2006). Drunk in public, drunk in private: The relationship between college students, drinking environments and alcohol consumption. *The American Journal of Drug and Alcohol Abuse , 32* (2), 275-285.

Clary, B. J., Dolfsma, W., & Figart, D. M. (2006). *Ethics and the Market - Insight from social economics.* New York: Routledge.

Cobley, E. (2009). *Modernism and the Culture of Efficiency: Ideology and Fiction.* Toronto, Canada: University of Toronto Press Incorporated.

Collins, J. E. (1994). Is business ethics and oxymoron? *Business Horizons , 37* (5), 1-8.

Cormier, D., & Gordon, I. M. (2001). An examination of social and environmental reporting strategies . *Accounting, Auditing & Accountability Journal , 14*, 587-617.

Cowen, C., & Thompson, P. (1999). Ethical banking: Progress and prospects. *Financial Times* .

Cowton, C. J. (1994). The development of ethical investment products. In A. Prindl, & B. Prodhan, *Ethical Conflicts in Finance,* (pp. 213-232). Oxford: Blackwell.

Crane, A., & Matten, D. (2010). *Business ethics* (Vol. 3). Oxford: Oxford University Press.

Crotty, M. (1998). *The Foundations of Social Research: Meaning and Perspective in the Research Process.* London: Sage.

David, M., & Sutton, C. D. (2011). *Social Research: An introduction* (Vol. 2). London: Sage.

de Clerck, F. (2009). *Ethical banking.* Retrieved July 26, 2012 from http://www.social-banking.org/fileadmin/isb/Artikel_und_Studien/de_Clerck_Ethical_Banking.pdf

Denscombe, M. (2010). *The Good Research Guide* (Vol. 4). Maidenhead: McGraw-Hill Education.

Deutsche Bank. (2012, July 28). *Banking on Green.* Retrieved July 28, 2012 from http://www.banking-on-green.de/

Dias-Sardinha, L., Reijnders, L., & Antunes, P. (2007). Developing Sustainability Balanced Scorecards for Environmental Services: A Study of Three Large Portuguese Companies. *Environmental Quality Managemen , 16* (4), 13-34.

Die Zeit Online. (2012, July 2012). *"Lasst Banken pleitegehen".* Retrieved November 13, 2012 from http://www.zeit.de/politik/ausland/2012-06/kritik-euro-rettungskurs

Dolfsma, B. J., Figart, W., & Clary, D. (2011). *Ethics and the market - Insight from social economics.* New York: Routledge Chapman & Hall.

Donaldson, J. (1992). *Business Ethics: A European Casebook.* London: Academic Press.

Dworkin, R. M. (1977). *Taking Rights Seriously.* London: Duckworth.

Ecolabel Index. (2012, October 06). *Introducing Ecolabel Index.* Retrieved October 06, 2012 from http://www.ecolabelindex.com/

EFTA. (2012a, December 12). *EEA Agreement.* Retrieved December 12, 2012 from http://www.efta.int/eea/eea-agreement.aspx

EFTA. (2012b, December 12). *The European Free Trade Association.* Retrieved December 12, 2012 from http://www.efta.int/about-efta/the-european-free-trade-association.aspx

EIRIS. (2012, December 12). *About us.* Retrieved December 12, 2012 from http://www.eiris.org/about_us.html

EIRIS. (2007). *The EIRIS Green & Ethical Funds Directory.* London: EIRIS.

El País. (2011, September 11). *Ethical banking takes root in the mire of the global financial crisis.* Retrieved July 26, 2012 from http://elpais.com/elpais/2011/09/12/inenglish/1315804847_850210.html

Endress. (2012, December 09). *Waste Incineration Power Plants.* Retrieved December 09, 2012 from http://www.endress.com/eh/home.nsf/#page/~power-energy-processes-waste-incineration-power-plants

Ernst & Young. (2011). *Global Consumer Banking Survey 2011.* Retrieved July 23, 2012 from http://www.ey.com/GL/en/Industries/Financial-Services/Banking---Capital-Markets/Global-banking-survey--a-new-era-of-customer-expectation---Rebuild-brand-perception

European Commission. (2012, September 25). *Ecolabel*. Retrieved September 25, 2012 from http://ec.europa.eu/environment/ecolabel/

European Commission. (2012, February). *Europeans and their Languages.* Retrieved December 09, 2012 from Special Eurobarometer 386 / Wave EB77.1 Special Eurobarometer: http://ec.europa.eu/public_opinion/archives/ebs/ebs_386_en.pdf

European Commission. (2012, October 1). *Policies*. Retrieved October 1, 2012 from http://ec.europa.eu/policies/index_en.htm

European Communities. (1997). *Treaty of Amsterdam.* Luxembourg: Office for Official Publications of the European Communities,.

European Parliament . (2000, December 04). *Directive 2000/76/EC of the European Parliament and of the Council of 4 December 2000 on the incineration of waste*. Retrieved December 09, 2012 from http://eur-lex.europa.eu/LexUriServ/LexUriServ.do?uri=CELEX:32000L0076:EN:NOT

FairTrade International. (2012, July 27). *What is Fairtrade?* Retrieved July 27, 2012 from http://www.fairtrade.net/what_is_fairtrade.html

FEBEA. (2012a, April 17). *What really differentiates ethical banks from traditional banks?* Retrieved October 06, 2012 from http://www.ethicalbankingeurope.com/sites/default/files/Definition%20Ethical%20Bank.pdf

FEBEA. (2012b, December 12). *Why FEBEA?* Retrieved December 12, 2012 from http://www.febea.org/why_febea.php

Femu qui. (2012, November 14). *Comment intervenons nous?* Retrieved November 14, 2012 from http://www.femu-qui.com/Comment-intervenons-nous_a11.html

Ferrell, O. C., & Gresham, L. G. (1985). A contingency framework for understanding ethical decision making in marketing. *Journal of Marketing , 49*, 87-98.

Ferrell, O. C., Fraedrich, J., & Ferrell, L. (2008). *Business Ethics: Ethical Decision Making & Cases.* Mason: South-Western Cengage Learning.

Ferrell, O. C., Fraedrich, J., & Ferrell, L. (2010). *Business Ethics: Ethical Decision Making & Cases* (Vol. 7). Mason: South-Western Cengage Learning.

Fisher, C., & Lovell, A. (2009). *Business Ethics and Values* (Vol. 3). Harlow: Prentice Hall.

Ford, H. (1903). *Ford Motor Company Fund & Community Services.* Retrieved July 29, 2012 from http://corporate.ford.com/our-company/community/ford-fund/presidents-message-401p?releaseId=1244754314736

Freeman, R. E. (1984). *Strategic Management - A Stakeholder Approach.* London: Pitman.

French, R., Rayner, C., Rees, G., & Rumbles, S. (2005). *Organizational Behaviour* (Vol. 2). Chichester: John Wiley & Sons.

Gee, D. (2001). *Business and the environment: current trends and developments in corporate reporting and ranking* . European Environment Agency. Copenhagen: European Environment Agency.

Gerrans, P., & Hutchinson, B. (2000). Sustainable Development and Small and Medium-Sized Enterprises: A Long Way to Go. In R. Hillary, *Small and Medium-Sized Enterprises and the Environment: Business Imperatives* (pp. 75-82). Sheffield, UK: Greenleaf Publishing Limited.

Giuseppi, J. (2001). Assessing the 'Triple bottom line' - Social and environmental practices in the European banking sector. In J. J. Bouma, M. Jeucken, & L. Klinkers, *Sustainable Banking - The greening of finance* (pp. 96-112). Sheffield, UK: Greenleaf Publishing Limited.

Global Environmental Governance Project. (2012, February 11). *Debate Over UNEP's Future Continues.* Retrieved October 03, 2012 from http://www.environmentalgovernance.org/featured/2012/02/debate-over-uneps-future-continues/

Global Reporting Initiative. (2010/2011). *A new phase: the growth of sustainability reporting.* Amsterdam: GRI.

Global Sustainable Tourism Council. (2012, July 27). *GSTC Accredited Program.* Retrieved July 27, 2012 from http://www.gstcouncil.org/resource-center/gstc-approval-process-for-standards-and-certification-programs/program-gstc-accredited.html

Goethe Institut. (2008, March). *Sustainability – From Principle To Practice.* Retrieved October 03, 2012 from http://www.goethe.de/ges/umw/dos/nac/den/en3106180.htm

Goff, S. (2011, June 15). *Ethical banking: Strong principles foster growth.* (Financial Times UK) Retrieved October 01, 2012 from Financial Times UK: http://www.ft.com/cms/s/0/93502918-9716-11e0-9c9d-00144feab49a.html#axzz2846cG43Q

Goodpaster, K. E. (1983). The concept of Corporate Responsibility. *Journal of Business Ethics , 1*, 1-22.

Google. (2012, November 06). *Google Docs - Forms*. Retrieved November 06, 2012 from https://sites.google.com/a/share.epsb.ca/learning-with-web-2-0-technology--lwt-aisi/Home/voki

Goyal, K. A., & Joshi, V. (2011). A study of social and ethical issues in banking industry. *International Journal of Economic Research , II* (5), 49-57.

Grace, D., & Cohen, S. (2010). *Business ethics* (Vol. 4). Oxford: Oxford University Press.

Green, C. F. (1989). Business Ethics in Banking. *Journal of Business Ethics* (3), 1-4.

Gros, D., & Mayer, T. (2010). *How to deal with sovereign default in Europe.* Brussels: Center for European Policy Studies.

Guttmacher Institute. (2012, December 09). *Facts on Induced Abortion Worldwide*. Retrieved December 09, 2012 from http://www.guttmacher.org/pubs/fb_IAW.html

Hamel, G., & Prahalad, C. K. (1994). *Competing for the future.* Columbus: Mcgraw-Hill Professional.

Hart, C. (2005). *Doing your Masters Dissertation.* London: Sage.

Henriques, A., & Richardson, J. (2004). *The triple bottom line: Does it all add up?* London: Earthscan.

Hoffmann, E. (2003). *Environmental Reporting and Sustainability Reporting in Europe.* IGES Kansai Research Center. Maastricht: University of Maastricht.

Hughes, G., Mayo, E., & Lake, R. (1999). *European bank's environmental and social policies and business practices survey.* National provident institution. Peterborough: Global Care.

Hunt, S. D., & Vitell, S. (1986). A General Theory of Marketing Ethics. *Journal of Macromarketing , 6*, 5-16.

Institut der deutschen Wirtschaft Köln. (2011). Lohnt sich Nachhaltigkeit? *Wirtschaft und Ethik* (3), 1-4.

Institute of Islamic Banking and Insurance. (2012, October 02). *Shari'ah Supervisory Board [Religious Board].* Retrieved October 02, 2012 from http://www.islamic-banking.com/takaful_shariah_supervisory_board.aspx

International Energy Agency. (2010). *2010 Key World Energy Statistics.* Paris: International Energy Agency.

Ioannou, I., & Serafeim, G. (2012). *The Consequences of Mandatory Corporate Sustainability Reporting.* Harvard Business School.

Janda, K., Berry, J. M., Goldman, J., & Hula, K. W. (2009). *The challange of democracy* (Vol. 2). Boston: Wadsworth Cengage Learning.

Jeucken, M. (1998). Duurzaam bankieren. *Bank- en Effectenbedrijf* (10), 17-21.

Jeucken, M. (2002). Slow starters are gaining pace - The response of banks to sustainability issues. *International Financial Institutions* (2), 12-16.

Jeucken, M. (2002). *Sustainable Finance and Banking - The Financial Sector and the Future of the Planet.* London, UK: Earthscan Publications Ltd.

Jeucken, M., & Bouma, J. J. (1999). The changing environment of banks. *GMGreener Management International: The Journal of Corporate Environmental Strategy and Practice* (Winter), 21-35.

Kitson, A. (1996). Taking the pulse: Ethics and the British Cooperative Bank. *Journal of Business Ethics* (15), 1021-1031.

Kleanthous, A., & Peck, J. (2006). *Let them eat cake - Satisfying the new consumer appetite for responsible brands.* Godalming: WWF.

KPMG Australia. (2008). *Sustainable Reporting*. Melbourne: KPMG Australia & The Group of 100.

KPMG. (2011). *KPMG International Survey of Corporate Responsibility Reporting 2011*. KPMG.

KPMG. (1999). *KPMG International Survey of Environmental Reporting 1999.* University of Amsterdam, Institute for Environmental Management (WIMM). De Meern: KPMG.

Kumar, R. (2011). *Research Methodology - a step-by-step guide for beginners* (Vol. 3). London: SAGE Publications Ltd.

Lee, C. C., & Yang, J. (2000). Emerald Article: Knowledge value chain. *Journal of Management Development , 19* (9), pp. 783-794.

Lloyds. (2012). *Lloyds Banking Group Responsible Business Report 2011.* London: Lloyds Banking Group.

Lober, D. J., Bynum, D., Campbell, E., & Jacques, M. (1997). The 100 plus corporate environmental report study: A survey of an evolving environmental management tool. *Business Strategy and the environment , 6*, 57-73.

Mätäsaho, R., & Niskala, M. (1997, January). Ympäristölaskentatoimi. *LTA* , 76-91.

Marimuthu, M., Jing, C. W., Gie, L. P., Mun, L. P., & Ping, T. Y. (2010). Islamic Banking: Selcetion Criteria and Implications. *Global Journal of Human Social Science , 10* (4), 52-62.

McDermott, L. J., Dobson, A., & Owen, N. (2006). From partying to parenthood: young women's perceptions of cigarette smoking across life transitions. *Health Education Research , 21* (3), 428-439.

Meadowcroft, J. (2007). National Sustainable Development Strategies: Features, Challenges and Reflexivity. *European Environment , 17*, 152-163.

Melrose-Woodman, J. E., & Kverndal, I. (1976). *Towards Social Responsibility: Company Codes of Ethics and Practice*. London: British Institute of Management.

Mizzoni, J. (2010). *Ethics - The Basics*. Oxford: Blackwell Publishing.

Mukras, M. S. (1993). *Elementary Econometrics.* Nairobi: East African Educational Publishers Ltf.

Mulder, I. (2007). *Biodiversity, the next challange for financial institutions?* Gland, Switzerland: IUCN.

OECD. (2012, December 12). *UNEP.* Retrieved December 12, 2012 from http://stats.oecd.org/glossary/detail.asp?ID=2803

Olsthoorn, X., Tyteca, D., Wehrmeyer, W., & Wagner, M. (2000, November). Environmental indicators for business: A review of the literature and standardisation methods. *Journal of Cleaner Production* .

O'Rourke, A. (2003). The message and method of ethical investments. *Journal of Cleaner Production , 11* (6), 683-693.

Paliwal, M. (2007). *Business Ethics.* New Delhi: New Age International.

Polit, D., & Hungler, B. (1999). *Nursing research: Principles and methods* (Vol. 6). Philadelphia: Lippincott.

Robbins, P. (2001). *Greening the corporation - Management strategy and the environmental challenge.* London, UK: Earthscan.

Robson, C. (2002). *Real World Research* (Vol. 2). Oxford: Blackwell.

Rodríguez Parada, S. M., & Cabaleiro Casal, M. (2007). El compromiso social de la banca alternativa. *Ekonomiaz* (65), 228-259.

Russell, B., & Purcell, J. (2009). *Online Research Essentials.* San Francisco: John Wiley & Sons.

Ryan, A. B. (2006). Post-positivist Approaches to Research. In M. Antonsa, H. Fallon, A. B. Ryan, & T. Walsh (Eds.), *Researching and Writing your Thesis: A Guide for Postgraduate Students* (pp. 12-28). Maynooth: MACE.

Sörensen, P. (2001). Foreword. In J. J. Bouma, M. Jeucken, & L. Klinkers, *Sustainable Banking - The Greening of finance.* Sheffield: Greenleaf Publishing Limited.

San-Jose, L., Retolaza, J. L., & Gutierrez-Goiria, J. (2011). Ethical Banks: An Alternative in the Financial Crisis. *Journal of Business Ethics , 100* (1), 151-173.

Saunders, M., Lewis, P., & Thornhill, A. (2012). *Research methods for business students* (Vol. 6). Harlow: Pearson Education Limited.

Schlegelmilch, B. B., & Houston, J. E. (1989). Corporate Codes of Ethics in Large UK Companies: An Empirical Investigation of Use, Content and Attitudes. *European Journal of Marketing , 23*, 7-24.

Schmidheiny, S., & Zorraquin, F. J. (1996). *Financing Change: the Financial Community, Ecoefficiency, and Sustainable Development.* Massachusetts, US: MIT Press.

Sevilla, C. G., Ochave, J. A., Punsalan, T. G., Regala, B. P., & Uriarte, G. G. (2007). *Research Methods.* Quezon City: Rex Printing Company.

Skillius , Å., & Wennberg, U. (1998). *Continuity, Credibility and Comparability.* Lund University, The International Institute for Industrial Environmental Economics. Lund: European Environment Agency.

Solé, J. (2007). Introducing Islamic Banks into Conventional Banking Systems. *IMF Working Paper , 07* (175).

Spiegel Online. (2009, August 01). *Katholische Bank investiert in Verhütungsmittel-Hersteller.* Retrieved October 02, 2012 from http://www.spiegel.de/panorama/gesellschaft/ethische-anlagen-katholische-bank-investiert-in-verhuetungsmittel-hersteller-a-639733.html

Stahlmann, V., & Clausen, J. (2000). *Umweltleistung von Unternehmen: Von der Öko-Effizienz zur Öko-Effektivität.* Wiesbaden, Germany: Gabler Verlag.

Stern. (2009, August 01). *Katholische Bank investiert - in Verhütung.* Retrieved October 02, 2012 from http://www.stern.de/panorama/pax-bank-katholische-bank-investiert-in-verhuetung-707854.html

Stigson, B. (1999). What is Eco-Efficiency? The WBCSD perspective. *Roundtable on Eco-Efficiency* (pp. 1-7). Sydney: WBCSD.

Street, P., & Monaghan, P. (2011). Assessing the sustainability of bank service channels - The case of the Co-operative bank. In J. J. Bouma, M. Jeucken, & L. Klinkers, *Sustainable Banking* (pp. 72-87). Sheffield, UK: Greenleaf Publishing Limited.

Tapscott, D. (2009). *Grown Up Digital: How the Net Generation is Changing Your World.* New York: McGraw-Hill.

Tarna, K. (2001). Reporting on the environment. In J. J. Bouma, M. Jeucken, & L. Klinkers, *Sustainable Banking* (pp. 149-165). Sheffield: Greenleaf Publishing Ltd.

Taylor, J. W. (1975). *Principles of ethics: An introduction to ethics* (Vol. 1). Encino: Dickenson.

The American Heritage Dictionary. (2006). *The American Heritage Dictionary of the English language* (Vol. 4). Boston: Houghton Mifflin Company.

The Blue Angel. (2012, September 25). *Welcome to the Blue Angel*. Retrieved September 25, 2012 from http://www.blauer-engel.de/en/index.php

Thomas, L. B. (2006). *Money, Banking and Financial Markets.* Masion, Ohio: South-Western.

Tomorrow. (1993, July). Banking on the Planet. *Tomorrow* , 32-34.

UBS. (2011). *Code of Business Conduct and Ethics of UBS.* Zurich: UBS.

UNEP. (2012a, December 12). *A world of development experience*. Retrieved December 12, 2012 from http://www.undp.org/content/undp/en/home/operations/about_us.html

UNEP Finance Initiative. (2012b, October 03). *Our Members*. Retrieved October 03, 2012 from http://www.unepfi.org/signatories/index.html

UNEP. (2012c, December 12). *News*. Retrieved December 12, 2012 from http://www.unep.org/

UNICEF. (2007). *Children and the Millenium Development Goals.* New York: United Nations Children's Fund.

United Nations. (2012, December 12). *What's Going On?* Retrieved December 12, 2012 from http://www.un.org/millenniumgoals/

United States Environmental Protection Agency. (2012, August 01). *CERCLA Overview*. Retrieved August 01, 2012 from http://www.epa.gov/superfund/policy/cercla.htm

Wilson, R. (1997). Islamic finance and ethical investment. *International Journal of Social Economics , 24*, 1325-1342.

Wilson, R. (2002). Parallels between Islamic and Ethical Banking. *Review of Islamic Economics , 11*, 51-62.

Winlow, S., & Hall, S. (2011). What is an 'ethics committee'? *British Journal of Criminology* , *52*, 400-416.

World Commission on Environment and Development:. (1987). *Report of the World Commission on Environment and Development: Our Common Future.* Oslo: Worldbank.

World Health Organization. (2012, December 09). *Facts and figures about abortion in the European Region*. Retrieved December 09, 2012 from http://www.euro.who.int/en/what-we-do/health-topics/Life-stages/sexual-and-reproductive-health/activities/abortion/facts-and-figures-about-abortion-in-the-european-region

Wroe, A. (1965). *Dynamic Marketing Behaviour.* Homewood: Irwin.

Yale Center for Environmental Law & Policy. (2012). *EPI 2012 - Environmental Performance Index and Pilot Trend Environmental Performance Index.* New Haven: Yale University.

YourEthicalMoney.org. (2012, December 12). *Home*. Retrieved December 12, 2012 from http://www.yourethicalmoney.org/

VII Appendix A

1 Survey about ethical banks

1.1 Introduction

Thank you for choosing to participate in my survey on 'Ethical Banks'.
Please note that all data collected will only be used in the scope of this project and will be treated confidentially.
Answering all survey question will approximately take between 5 to 10 minutes.
Thank you for taking your time!

1.2 Personal information

1.2.1 Please indicate your sex:

Male	43
Female	53

1.2.2 Please indicate your age:

0 - 20	16
20 - 30	32
30 - 40	24
40 - 50	9
50 - 65	11
65 - 100	4

1.2.3 In which country do you live?

Austria	5
Belgium	2
Bulgaria	0
Cyprus	0
Czech Republic	2

Denmark	3
Estonia	2
Finland	1
France	6
Germany	11
Greece	1
Hungary	2
Iceland	0
Ireland	5
Italy	3
Latvia	1
Liechtenstein	1
Lithuania	2
Luxembourg	3
Malta	0
Netherlands	4
Norway	2
Poland	6
Portugal	3
Romania	1
Slovakia	1
Slovenia	0
Spain	6
Sweden	3
Switzerland	4
United Kingdom	12

Other	4

1.3 Banking habits

1.3.1 Which of the following statements reflects your banking habits best?

I do not have any bank products.	1
I have all my bank products (current account, savings account, loans, etc.) at one main (primary) bank.	36
I have my bank products spread between two banks.	39
I have my bank products spread between three or more banks.	20

1.3.2 How many bank products do you approximately own?

0	1
1	12
2	12
3	15
4	24
5	12
6	12
7	2
8	4
9	1
10	1

1.3.3 Do you plan on changing your main bank soon?

Yes	82
No	14

1.3.3.1 If yes, please indicate why in the field below:

- My bank allows you to close a bank account without even showing proof of ID, don't like that.
- I finished my Bachelor right now...so my old main bank will spread my free current account in a few weeks.
- Bad service, low time for response on inquiries or problem solving. Saturated banks as there is always so many people in the bank. Terrible efficiency.
- I am moving to a different country.
- Bad service.
- No knowledge.
- The branches are too far away from where I live at the moment.
- Bad service.
- I had an argument with my bank adviser.
- The service standard is really low.
- Unfriendly customer service.
- Banking is only possible by appointment.
- No polite behaviour.

1.3.4 Have you ever heard of the term 'ethical bank'?

Yes	42
No	54

1.3.4.1 If 1.3.4 is answered with yes: Do you have a banking account with a supposedly ethical bank?

Yes	8
No	20
Not sure	14

1.3.4.1.1 If 1.3.4.1 is answered with yes: Please write down the name of the bank.

- HSBC
- GLS Bank
- Crédal
- Cultura Sparebank
- ETIKA
- Valartis Bank
- TISE
- Ethik Bank

1.3.4.2 If 1.3.4 If answered with yes: Even though you might not consider your bank as ethical, do you know if your bank offers ethical products, respectively accounts?

Yes	5
No	29
Not sure	8

1.3.4.2.1 If 1.3.4.2 is answered with yes: Please write down the name of the bank and ethical products the bank offers.

- Erste Bank
- Estonian Credit Union
- Deutsche Bank
- Banco Espirito Santo
- HSBC Bank Czech

1.3.5 Have you ever heard of the term 'Islamic Banking'?

Yes	53
No	43

1.3.5.1 If 1.3.5 is answered with yes: Do you have a bank account with an Islamic Bank?

Yes	4
No	49

1.3.5.1.1 If 1.3.5.1 is answered with yes: Please write down the name of the bank you are conducting Islamic Banking with:

- Alrajhi
- Dubai Islamic Bank
- Denmark Islamic Bank
- Islamic Bank of Britain

1.3.5.1.2 If 1.3.5.1 is answered with no: Would you consider investing in Islamic bank accounts? Which of the following statements reflects your view on Islamic Banking products?

Even though I am not a Muslim, I do like the concept of Islamic Banks and would consider them in the future.	8
I am a Muslim and required by Sharia law to solely use these products.	0
I am not a Muslim. Hence, I will not conduct any financial transactions with an Islamic Bank.	15
Even though I am a Muslim, I am using non-Islamic banks only.	9
I am not a Muslim, but don't care if it is an Islamic or non-Islamic bank that carries out my financial transactions.	17
I am a Muslim and would conduct my financial transactions with banks that offer the best terms and conditions, regardless whether they are Sharia or non-Sharia compliant.	0
I don't want to answer this question.	0

1.3.6 Which of the following statements reflects your view on sustainability?

I am absolutely aware of global environmental and social issues and I always act in the best way possible to protect the environment and to contribute vitally to the social stability of our community.	24
I recognise that there are environmental and social issues surrounding me and I try to include them as often as possible when making decisions.	50
I do understand that there are environmental and social issues in our society, but I rarely think about theses issues when making decisions.	17
I care neither about the environment nor other people around me.	5

1.4 Ethical criteria

In the following questions you are asked to give your opinion on environmental and social topics with respect to ethics.

Which of the following criteria do you consider as ethical?

Please indicate your opinion according to the following scale:

1. I agree strongly that this criterion is ethical.
2. I agree to some extend that it this criteria is ethical.
3. I am undecided whether it is ethical or not.
4. It applies to a lesser extend ethical to me.
5. It doesn't apply to me as ethical at all.

1.4.1 Leisure and entertainment (Sale and production)

Do you consider the following criteria as ethical?

	Agree strongly	Agree to some extend	Undecided	Applies to a lesser extend	Doesn't apply at all
Alcohol	9	19	24	36	8
Tobacco	5	23	28	31	9
Pornography	0	0	21	32	38
Adult Entertainment Services	5	19	21	28	14
Gambling	5	4	33	33	16
Coffee-Shops (NL)	8	38	16	10	14

1.4.2 Animals and plants

Do you consider the following criteria as ethical?

	Agree strongly	Agree to some extend	Undecided	Applies to a lesser extend	Doesn't apply at all
Animal testing	8	22	0	19	42
Animal disposal industry	4	23	17	13	34
Fishing (MSC certified)	9	50	13	19	5

Development of alternative textiles to leather	23	41	17	10	0
Slaughterhouses	4	36	22	9	15
Dairy production	8	50	18	15	0
Fur trade	17	9	5	27	33
Sale of pork meat	18	21	28	10	14
Intensive farming	13	17	20	27	14
Animal welfare	33	27	4	17	5
Organic farming	37	36	9	0	4

1.4.3 Weapons

Do you consider the following criteria as ethical?

	Agree strongly	Agree to some extend	Undecided	Applies to a lesser extend	Doesn't apply at all
Military sales	13	9	4	31	29
Weapons used by the Military	4	13	5	46	24
Foreign Military Sales program	0	0	9	41	33
Private weapon industry	8	4	10	37	37
Sport shooting	5	18	32	22	19
Hunting weapons	4	27	9	33	23
Cluster bomb manufacturers	8	0	9	24	50
Landmines	12	5	5	9	55
Nuclear weapons	8	0	4	5	69

Biologic weapons	4	8	0	0	74
Chemical weapons	8	4	0	0	74
Energy weapons	8	4	0	0	74
Magnetic weapons	8	9	0	5	64
Paintball	18	27	19	34	0

1.4.4 Energy

Do you consider the following criteria as ethical?

	Agree strongly	Agree to some extend	Undecided	Applies to a lesser extend	Doesn't apply at all
Coal generated energy	8	32	19	28	5
Oil energy	22	43	13	9	0
Natural gas energy	8	28	34	13	5
Methane hydrate energy	60	22	0	5	4
Wind energy	41	28	13	5	4
Tidal energy	57	25	9	0	0
Energy efficient devices	50	27	5	4	0
Ocean stream energy	65	17	0	4	0
Energy by ocean waves	45	28	13	0	0
Osmosis energy	50	24	13	4	0
Photovoltaic energy	73	14	0	4	0
Solar energy	33	22	23	4	4
Biomass conversion	51	18	9	4	4
Geothermic energy	5	16	14	32	24
Nuclear power plants	9	27	32	10	13

Energy-intensive industries	20	17	33	13	13
Waste incineration plants	8	8	4	9	57
Radioactive waste	4	32	23	32	0
Energy-intensive material production (e.g. Steel, cement, ...)	4	23	24	22	18
Thermic energy of the spontaneous nuclear disintegration	37	42	12	0	0
Drinking water purification	37	46	4	0	4
Waste water treatment	51	18	8	9	0
Waste reduction	59	18	8	9	0
Recycling	8	26	14	19	24

1.4.5 Medical and pharmaceuticals

Do you consider the following criteria as ethical?

	Agree strongly	Agree to some extend	Undecided	Applies to a lesser extend	Doesn't apply at all
Genetic modification of plants and seeds	4	30	27	20	10
Embryonic stem cell research	9	32	27	9	14
Holistic therapies	8	41	19	14	9
Life termination (Arbortion, assisted suicide, etc.)	23	38	18	4	8
Alternative medicine	13	46	28	4	0

Vaccine development	4	22	18	18	25
Manufacturing or supplying ozone-depleting chemicals	35	42	14	0	0
Care homes	50	27	14	0	0
Hospitals	13	21	33	14	10
Human genetic engineering	12	21	34	14	10
Pharmaceutical companies in general	18	40	29	4	5
Pharmaceutical companies (except if demonstrating an outstanding positive response towards environmental and social concerns)	8	37	14	9	18
Xenotransplantation (transplanting organs from animals to humans)	13	19	36	5	9
Connection to countries with health and safety offenses	13	15	36	13	9
Companies with health and safety offenses	12	24	13	28	14
Payment of medical test candidates	37	32	14	4	4
Organ donations	41	33	13	4	0
Blood donations	17	34	18	22	5
Aesthetic surgery	13	43	21	9	0

1.4.6 Commodities

Do you consider the following criteria as ethical?

	Agree strongly	Agree to some extend	Undecided	Applies to a lesser extend	Doesn't apply at all
Commodities from developing countries	23	41	9	9	0
Regeneration	4	32	31	10	19
Tropical hardwood	5	26	32	18	15
Mining	28	36	24	4	4
Conventional Agriculture	12	10	9	55	10
Oil industry	8	18	23	19	23
Unsustainable timber industry	8	42	17	24	5
Paper companies	12	19	14	14	32
Deforestation of primary forest	12	19	9	10	36
Deforestation of virgin forests	18	36	33	9	0
FSC certified forestry	4	18	27	19	18
Unsustainable commodities	8	19	22	14	24
Diamond industry	17	29	9	32	9

1.4.7 Transportation

Do you consider the following criteria as ethical?

	Agree strongly	Agree to some extend	Undecided	Applies to a lesser extend	Doesn't apply at all
Automobile industry	4	42	17	23	5
Freight traffic	13	37	22	14	5
Mass transit systems	12	41	23	15	5
Logistic companies	8	14	59	10	5
Road haulage companies	4	41	36	0	5
Maritime industry	17	29	31	9	0
Road building (<10% of turnover)	68	14	4	0	0
Bicycles	17	42	27	0	0
Motorbikes	55	27	0	4	0
Electric vehicle	17	43	5	26	0
Air travel industry	8	10	5	4	51

1.4.8 Law, International Agreements, Corporate Governance

Do you consider the following criteria as ethical?

	Agree strongly	Agree to some extend	Undecided	Applies to a lesser extend	Doesn't apply at all
Child labour	28	36	5	5	4
Compliance with labour rights	37	27	5	5	4
UN Human rights policy	28	35	15	5	0

Convention of the International Labour Organization	18	46	9	5	0
Conviction of serious pollution by Environmental Agency	23	47	0	8	0
Compliance with environmental policies	0	15	12	12	39
No equal opportunities policy	0	27	13	19	24
Violation of standards by the Advertising Standards Authority (e.g. broke the international code of breast milk substitutes developing countries)	0	23	12	5	38
Support of any radical parties	0	18	37	14	9
Being present in countries that have not ratified the Kyoto-Protocol	0	27	24	23	9
Being present in countries that have not ratified the UNEP's Biodiversity Convention	0	23	29	22	14
Being present in countries considered as tax havens	0	28	24	22	9
Being present in countries that are not free according to the Freedom House Index (Azerbaijan,	5	18	32	19	9

Belarus, Cuba, Egypt, Kazakhstan, …)					
Being present in countries that are only party free according to the Freedom House Index (Albania, Armenia, Bolivia, Ecuador, Macedonia, Mexico, Thailand, …)	5	26	23	14	15
Being present in countries that enforce death penalty	4	14	15	13	32
Use of bribery	4	14	15	14	32
Being present in countries that are corrupt (Rating < 4 of the Corruption Perceptions Index)	4	23	15	22	19
Being present in countries that have an oppressive regime	9	9	24	18	23
Being present in countries that have an undemocratic regime	5	9	31	15	23
Violation of civil rights	4	9	15	17	33
Support right of privacy	22	42	5	4	5
Environmental reporting	27	38	14	4	0
Disclosure and transparency of data	31	37	5	5	0
Sound corporate governance policies	23	37	14	4	0
Policies for employees	24	45	9	0	0

Compliance procedures for employees	19	40	14	0	0
Environmental management system	19	36	18	5	0
Respond fully to external enquiries	19	31	28	0	0
Code of conduct available	13	42	19	0	0
Social audits	23	37	14	4	0
Monitoring of policies	23	36	10	9	0
Business ethics statement	14	42	19	8	0
Continuous improvement of sustainable activities	19	45	19	0	0
Safety system within a company	33	40	10	0	0

1.4.9 Finance and support

Do you consider the following criteria as ethical?

	Agree strongly	Agree to some extend	Undecided	Applies to a lesser extend	Doesn't apply at all
Political donations	8	23	10	27	19
Being exposed to large company debt	4	17	29	23	10
Being exposed to Third World Debt	4	13	22	24	15
Investments in financial institutions	4	28	41	14	0
Refugee aid	33	45	14	0	0

Educational support	46	27	10	4	0
Donations to charities	47	23	8	9	0
Scholarships	47	27	5	4	0
Accounts for small businesses	38	49	0	0	0
Accounts for low income households	32	46	9	0	0
Support of community initiatives	37	41	0	5	0
Employee benefits	28	54	5	0	0
Family friendly benefits	33	45	4	0	5
Complementary healthcare	26	45	5	0	5
Microcredits	22	37	18	0	5
Pregnancy support	38	44	0	5	0
Maternity / Paternity leave	42	26	5	4	5
Maintaining a check and balance system for operations	19	46	22	0	0
Fundraising	24	41	17	5	0
Employee share ownership plan	37	37	9	4	0
Nursing services	50	27	5	0	5
Care for elderly	46	31	10	0	0
Counselling services	28	45	14	0	0
Promotion of sustainable lifestyle among all ages	40	37	5	5	0
Providing property for	46	28	9	4	0

social benefit					
Wide access to financial services	22	47	14	4	0
Support for companies that are integrating sustainable activities	23	55	0	0	9
Employee welfare	42	36	9	0	0

1.5 Thank you!

Thank you for participating in my online-survey!

If you have any further questions, comments or wish to leave feedback, please use the indicated field below.

Name:

Email address:

Comment:

VIIIAppendix B

1 Banks and investment funds used as a basis for extracting ethical criteria

1.1 Banks

Bank	Company Values / Code of Conduct	(N)egative and (P)ositive Criteria	Disclosure of supported projects (Detailed/General)	Ethical Committee
Andelskassen Oikos (Denmark)	X	P&N		
Merkur Andelskassen (Denmark)	X		G	
Folkesparekassen (Denmark)	X			
GLS Bank (Germany)	X	P&N		
Ethik Bank (Germany)	X	P&N		
UmweltBank (Germany)	X	P&N		
Triodos Bank (Netherlands)	X	P&N	D	
Fiare Banca Ètica (Spain)	X		G	
Coop57 (Spain)	X			
Charity Bank (United Kingdom)	X		D	
Co-operative Bank (United Kingdom)	X			X
Unit Trust Bank (United Kingdom)	X	P&N		
Ecology Building Society (United Kingdom)	X		D	
Cultura Bank (Norway)	X	P		
MagNet Community Bank (Hungary)	X			

Ekobanken (Sweden)	X		G	
La NEF (France)	X			
Alternative Bank Schweiz (Switzerland)	X			
Banca Popolare Etica (Italy)	X			
ASN Bank (Netherlands)	X	N&P		
Bank für Sozialwirtschaft (Germany)	X			
Caisse Solidaire du Nord-Pas-de-Calais (France)	X			X
Colonya Caixa Pollença (Spain)	X	N&P		
Etimos (Italy)	X		G	
Femu qui (France/Corsica)	X		D	
Hefboom (Belgium)	X			X
Sidi (France)	X		D	
Cassa Centrale Banca (Italy)	X			

1.2 Investment funds

1. Aberdeen Ethical Engagement UK Fund
2. Aberdeen Ethical World Fund
3. Aegon Ethical Cautious Managed Fund
4. Aegon Ethical Corporate Bond Fund
5. Aegon Ethical Equity Fund
6. Allchurches Amity Fund
7. AXA UK Ethical Fund
8. Banner Real Life Fund
9. Barchester Best of Green Life Fund
10. Barchester Best of Green Life Offshore Fund
11. Barchester Best of Green Pension Fund
12. CIS FTSE4Good Tracker Fund
13. CIS Sustainable Leaders Trust

14. Credit Suisse Fellowship Fund
15. Credit Suisse Multi Manager Ehical Fund
16. Direct Line FTSE4Good Tracker Fund
17. F&C Ethical Bond Fund
18. F&C Global Climate Opportunities Fund
19. F&C Stewardship Growth Fund
20. F&C Stewardship Income Fund
21. F&C Stewardship International Fund
22. Family Charities Ethical Trust
23. Friends Provident Stewardship Income Life Fund
24. Friends Provident Stewardship International Life Fund
25. Friends Provident Stewardship Life Fund
26. Friends Provident Stewardship Managed Life Fund
27. Friends Provident Stewardship Managed Pension Fund
28. Friends Provident Stewardship Safeguard Optimiser Fund
29. Halifax Ethical Fund
30. Henderson Global Care Growth Fund
31. Henderson Global Care Income Fund
32. Henderson Global Care Managed Fund
33. Henderson Industries of the Future Fund
34. Homeowners Friendly Society FTSE4Good Fund
35. HSBC Amanah Global Equity Index Fund
36. HSBC GIF Sustainability Leaders Fund
37. Impax Environmental Markets Investment Trust
38. Impax Environmental Markets OEIC
39. Insight Investment Ethical Fund
40. Insight Investment Evergreen Fund
41. Jupiter Ecology Fund
42. Jupiter Environmental Income Fund
43. Jupiter Global Green Investment Trust
44. King & Shaxson Ethical Balanced Income Fund
45. King & Shaxson Green Solutions Fund
46. Legal & General Ethical Pension Fund
47. Legal & General Ethical Trust
48. Lincoln Green Life Fund

49. Marks & Spencer Ethical fund
50. Marlborough Ethical Fund
51. Merchant Investors Assurance Ethical Cautious Managed Fund
52. Norwich Sustainable Future Absolute Growth Fund
53. Norwich Sustainable Future Corporate Bond Fund
54. Norwich Sustainable Future European Growth Fund
55. Norwich Sustainable Future Global Growth Fund
56. Norwich Sustainable Future Managed Fund
57. Norwich Sustainable UK Growth Fund
58. Norwich Union Ethical UK Equity Fund
59. Old Mutual Ethical Fund
60. Prudential Ethical Trust
61. Quadris Environmental Fund
62. Rathbone Ethical Bond Fund
63. Royal London Ethical Bond Trust
64. Schroders Global Climate Change
65. Scottish Widows Environmental Investor Fund
66. Scottish Widows Ethical Fund
67. Skandia Ethical Fund
68. Sovereign Ethical Fund
69. Standard Life Ethical Corporate Bond Fund
70. Standard Life Ethical Life Fund
71. Standard Life European Equity Ethical Fund
72. Standard Life Pension Ethical Fund
73. Standard Life UK Ethical Fund
74. SVM AllEurope SRI Fund
75. SWIP Global SRI Fund
76. SWIP Islamic Global Equity Fund
77. SWIP Pan-European SRI Equity Fund